HOME
FRONTS

OTHER BOOKS BY JESS WELLS

The Price of Passion
Lip Service (editor)
Lesbians Raising Sons (editor)
AfterShocks
Two Willow Chairs
The Dress, The Cry, and a Shirt With No Seams
A Herstory of Prostitution in Western Europe
The Sharda Stories
Run

HOME
FRONTS
CONTROVERSIES IN NONTRADITIONAL PARENTING

EDITED BY JESS WELLS

 alyson books
los angeles | new york

MANUFACTURED IN THE UNITED STATES OF AMERICA.

THIS TRADE PAPERBACK ORIGINAL IS PUBLISHED BY ALYSON PUBLICATIONS,
P.O. BOX 4371, LOS ANGELES, CA 90078-4371.
DISTRIBUTION IN THE UNITED KINGDOM BY
TURNAROUND PUBLISHER SERVICES LTD.,
UNIT 3, OLYMPIA TRADING ESTATE, COBURG ROAD, WOOD GREEN,
LONDON N22 6TZ ENGLAND.

FIRST EDITION: SEPTEMBER 2000

00 01 02 03 04 **a** 10 9 8 7 6 5 4 3 2 1

ISBN: 1-55583-532-5

LIBRARY OF CONGRESS CATALOGING-IN-PUBLICATION DATA
HOME FRONTS : CONTROVERSIES IN NONTRADITIONAL PARENTING /
EDITED BY JESS WELLS.
    ISBN 1-55583-532-5 (PBK)
    1. GAY PARENTS—UNITED STATES. 2. LESBIAN MOTHERS—UNITED
STATES. 3. GAY FATHERS—UNITED STATES. 4. CHILDREN OF GAY
PARENTS—UNITED STATES. I. WELLS, JESS.
HQ75.28.U6 H65 2000
306.874—DC21   00-032767

CREDITS
"FIRST, CLASS: ECONOMICS AND QUEER FAMILIES" BY TERRY BOGGIS WAS
    ORIGINALLY PRINTED IN THE COLUMBIA UNIVERSITY PUBLICATION *QUEER
    FAMILIES, QUEER POLITICS: CHALLENGING CULTURE AND THE STATE.*
"KATE KENDELL WANTS LESBIANS TO KEEP THEIR PROMISES" BY SARAH
    SCHULMAN WAS ORIGINALLY PUBLISHED IN *GIRLFRIENDS* MAGAZINE.
COVER DESIGN BY PHILIP PIROLO.

Dedicated to my son, Evan

Contents

Acknowledgments

I'd like to honor the tremendous courage and ingenuity of the lesbian, gay, bisexual, and transgender parenting community. Deepest thanks to Michele Karlsberg, publicist, manager, and friend; to Billie June Damon and Nora, Adele Prandini, Laurie Golub, Julie, John and Harold Wells, Nancy Bereano, Dan Biddle, Johnny, Cline, Michelle, and Barb. Many thanks for the insight and affection of Angela Brown and the fine people of Alyson. Special thanks to the Frau Doktor, for a second chance. And, as in all things, this is mostly for my son who, in his innocence, demands that I am a far better person than I ever thought I could be.

Introduction

Every nascent community focuses first on *how* to achieve its goals, leaving unspoken the *why* and, especially, any *oops*. In the case of the lesbian, gay, bisexual, and transgender (LGBT) parenting community, we have discussed how to get pregnant, how to gain our civil rights, how to legally protect ourselves. Only after we achieve a certain amount of safety and casualness about the mechanics of our lives are we able to step back and ask ourselves *why*, ask ourselves the tougher questions, examine the fallout of our decisions. Only after we secure a minimal amount of social stature are we able to realize that we've been painting a good face on our parenting and refusing to discuss our own mistakes because we've had to ward off the cultural assumption that we are all bad parents. When under siege, no one is capable of self-criticism.

The result, though, is that without this tough dialogue, the LGBT parenting community—like the lesbian community at large in the '70s or '80s, the "Sisterhood is Powerful" movement, or any other civil rights movement—has developed a reluctance to hear opposing voices. It has codified a mode of behavior that it has deemed correct. It has adopted patterns taken from the patriarchy in order to fit in and be accepted. It has relegated the tough questions to whispered conversations that begin with, "I know this isn't considered politically correct, but...."

We have achieved a lot in the last ten years, so it is with pride and a sense of our safety that I chose to embark on a book specifically focused on the controversies brewing within the LGBT parenting community. We are capable of withstanding a dialogue that doesn't focus on *how*, but on *how best*. The queer community has proven time and again that through these difficult conversations emerge wonderful ideas, groundbreaking concepts.

The writers in this book are longtime advocates of queer families; many have devoted decades to securing our rights and to coaching us into pregnancy, family building, and beyond—they offer unique perspectives based on extensive experience. Others write from an intensely personal level, describing issues that plague them and their children on a daily basis. Each has struggled through a sense of fear that their statements are heretical.

But the results, I think, are some excellent essays on the most critical issues in LGBT parenting today, many on topics that have never been discussed in any magazine or anthology. Terry Boggis, director of Center Kids in New York City, writes on class issues within the LGBT parenting community. Loree Cook-Daniels, a longtime advocate of the transgender community, offers an impassioned article on the reaction meted out to transgender parents. There are several voices, pro and con, on the heated topic of divorce and custody, including an interview with Kate Kendell by Sarah Schulman that goes beyond the typical issues as only Sarah can. Cindy Rizzo muses on biology, destiny, and divorce, while the rebuttal comes from Nom de Plum, who cautions us not to "bio–mom bash" by painting as villains all bio moms who deny custody to their ex-partners. Rachel Pepper struggles with the one-parent/two-parent quandary. Laurie Bell asks us to consider the connection between death and the rise in lesbian birthing during a time of AIDS. Judy Grahn, queer pioneer and one of our community's best minds, tackles the subject of matriarchal/matrilineal family structures. Aimee Gelnaw beautifully describes the pain of being a valuable family member who is, by biology, outside the circle of mother and child. LauRose Felicity provides a glimpse into a multiracial family and ties it, through stunning Southern language, to her own multiracial family of origin, while Arlene Istar Lev describes the struggle of bringing an African-American boy into a Jewish family. Tzivia Gover looks into the question of whether the sperm banks we're relying on are actually capable of connecting us with "willing-to-be-known" donors. Susie Bright takes a lighthearted jab at the naïveté of many lesbian parents, and I offer my own perspective on how parenting is changing lesbian culture.

This book also provides insight into extended-family constellations, such as James C. Johnstone's involvement as a donor dad; Kimberly Mistysyn's family with two moms and two dads; and Marcia Perlstein and James Hughson's experiences, as advocates, with the good and bad sides of lesbians and gay men building families together. Amity Pierce Buxton gives us a road map for dealing with hostile heterosexual ex-spouses, and Jenifer Firestone offers us a rare look from the 30,000-foot perspective of the state of the state of queer parenting.

The authors in this book were encouraged to push the limits, to write on the topics that kept them awake at night. If you find your own issue missing from this volume—as many issues are, admittedly—write. Produce a piece of fewer than

20 pages and E-mail it in Microsoft Word to jesswells@earth-link.net for possible inclusion in another volume. Without being apologetic, we offer these pieces not as the last word, but as the first of many—the opening salvo to begin a conversation that will free the LGBT community to question, to discuss, and, ultimately, to invent. It's an honor to be part of this dialogue, and I invite you to participate.

—Jess Wells
August 2000

The Essential Outsider: Life as the Non–Bio Mom
by Aimee Gelnaw

There *are* words to describe how I felt in the midst of my new daughter, Dewey, and my lover, Margie, during those first months of our lives together. Suddenly I found myself to be an outsider in my own family. The feelings were so consuming that I could not stop talking about them to the certain few who were able to hear me as I flailed about trying to comfort myself for the loss I felt at the birth our new baby. There were so many words yet so little comfort. Love makes a family, I thought.

In my work as an early-childhood educator I had been speaking (passionately and convincingly, I believed) on family diversity. I had written my master's thesis on how children intrinsically develop their own concept of family, thus shedding the notions that "family" is an externally imposed cultural construct and proving my hypothesis that the concept of family comes from within. I *expected* something different from my connection with Dewey. And I wanted it actualized, beginning at her birth. My life and work felt dependent upon it.

We create our families with so much to prove. From the

moment of my coming out and subsequent reconstructing of my family, I felt that my world of people (relationships both created and inherited) was in a constant state of holding its collective breath, anxiously awaiting the outcomes of our son, Zachary. I knew that deep down, despite my unwavering commitment to his well-being, others had a visceral wish for it to fail—proving, once and for all, there actually is only one prescribed way to make a family. And, after all, I had started this *experiment* with the perfect child—so noting his "spoilage" seemed the ideal opportunity to prove their point and go on comfortably, unquestioningly in their lives.

Zachary was born to me and my husband 11 years prior to Dewey's arrival. I had decided early on after Zachary's arrival on this earth that it doesn't get any better than this and that I was not going to tempt fate by having another child. I was delighted with him in every way. And the feeling was mutual.

When Margie and I began our life together around the time of Zack's fifth birthday, we did not impose her parenthood on him, and we carefully structured and cultivated an ongoing relationship with his father. In not much time Zack adopted Margie as his "stepmom," and she began to create a mothering relationship with him, gingerly taking cues from him and, I imagine, even more gingerly from me.

Margie frequently said that one of the things that most attracted her to me when we met was my mothering of Zack. She described our mother-child physical interactions as sensual and potent in a way she had not witnessed in my interactions with others. She applauded my abilities as a mother and enjoyed being amidst us in the symbiotic relationship Zack and I shared.

It was six more years until the birth of Dewey. Throughout those years Margie and Zack developed a relationship integral to each other's well-being and to the workings of the family. Margie struggled to keep the balance between her desire to move further in, while reading the cues for boundaries Zack intermittently imposed. I was the center of Zack's universe. And there grew in me a certain arrogance about this motherhood that I "shared" with Margie—not a purposeful arrogance, but an inevitable one. I did not have to do anything to create this power; Zack clearly sustained it on his own. And those in the outside world reinforced it with their thirst to prove their notions of the importance of biological connections (and for some—our allies—despite their desire not to do so, there remained the ingrained cultural assumptions that oozed out—deferring to me as "the mom" when they least expected it). It stubbornly, reassuringly, could not be undone. While Zack was clearly "ours" in numerous ways, he remained "mine" in many others.

For years Margie had made known her desire to bring a new baby into the family, but I was extremely reluctant. That it would happen was always a given. But my painful, nagging reluctance threw many hurdles into the process. I knew all too well how a baby had changed the relationship between me and Zack's father. These were frightening changes, the kind we feel alternately compelled to turn away from while stubbornly riveted to see, consequently hurling into question the dynamics of connection and belonging as we had understood them. Now, from a distance, I could see that these changes began at Zack's birth. Admitting this fear threatened to dismantle my self—the part of the self that's a mother and the part that believed in our family, Margie's and mine, as we currently knew it. It meant naming my ownership of Zack within the construct of our family of three and acknowledging the existence of an inner and outer circle in my own house. I was the one tirelessly working to convince others that love makes a family and that children unflinchingly respond to and create connections with those who love them, take care of them, and keep them safe. In my haste to feel affirmed in this connection, I was overlooking the *process of creating it*. Rather, I was feeling utterly entitled.

It all came down to such a primal response. Who will I be, and who will everyone else become in relationship to me? It's hard to admit, and I can't say I did admit it at the time, but we tirelessly talked about how this would be different because *I* was different than Zack's father and would be engaged and involved and spiritually connected. And we were doing this together. We nervously reviewed this each time we laid out another $1,000 in alternative-insemination expenses that stretched countlessly beyond the account we had created for this. And we discussed this in many other settings and situations, especially as we tried to convince others of what we were always convincing ourselves. Our commitment to having Dewey was clear in everything we did and said. We were possessed. For those who have experienced this whirlwind, I think you know what I mean. The desire for a lesbian couple to have a baby can be at times fraught with a weird concoction of drive, passion, rage, surrender, mystery, wonder, magic, and an endless array of powerful and unremitting feelings— many that we never planned on.

Once the pregnancy began, our attentions turned elsewhere. The idea of Dewey became the growing person Dewey. As she and Margie's body collaboratively grew and took on new form I became increasingly aware of the altering of our intimate life together. Gradually it began to feel like this life we shared became *lives*, as Dewey's size inserted itself between us. I grew achingly aware of a correlation between the expansion of Margie's physical self and an expansion of the physical gulf that separated us. I felt Margie grow further and further from reach—literally and emotionally.

As Dewey's in utero movements became consistent, I yearned for more than just the memory of the mother-fetus relationship, which I had known with Zack. I sometimes felt isolated and painfully aware that this relationship was Margie's experience and I was not within it; on the contrary, I was outside it, acting as the audience. It felt like a private party to which I could only remain peripheral. My engagement, no matter how attentive, could never replicate the one I'd felt during Zachary's prenatal life, nor could it ever equal that which Margie was experiencing with Dewey. My acute awareness of being an outsider ebbed and flowed throughout the pregnancy. It was not a terminal loss, but clearly a palpable one. I comforted myself with the anticipation of the external, holdable, tangible Dewey who would arrive after the birth. Then the scale would tip; the balance of commitment, passion, and relationship would pay off in the mutual connections we three would share. I was sure of it.

The tangible Dewey carved out an alarming presence in our household immediately upon her arrival. She was strong, intense, and, when unhappy, made you toil to regain calm and strive for moments of bliss. Conversely, she was charming, responsive, and engaging, and worth every effort. Margie was breast-feeding, and, as is inevitable, only she could be the source of the comfort and connection that comes from nursing. Indeed, as is the rhythm of life, Margie and Dewey were already connected. I grew to understand it as a connection that, for Dewey, had as its basis a lifetime of shared history beginning at conception. This is a history as visceral as the shared heartbeat, the rush and swoosh of blood flow, the reliability of breathing, the patter of voice, and all of the predictable, life-giving, and sustaining ways of being she could understand. Being held against Margie's chest conjured for her an aura of being "home" that could not be replicated by any other. They existed together in what, to me, felt like an impenetrable bubble. I remembered this existence well. I had lived in it years before with my son Zachary.

This phenomenon both fascinated and terrified me. I began to identify with the fathers I'd known over the years whom I'd faulted for lacking connection or engagement to their infant children. I wondered about the shifts occurring all too often in the husband-and-wife relationship as they take on the roles of mother and father. I felt complicit in Zack's father's compromised level of connection, which I perceived in their earliest attempts at relationship. I pitied my own father and the role of outsider to which he was relegated and remained in for a lifetime. I felt inexplicably but so fundamentally like them. I had seen but never *heard* some of these same pained experiences in other lesbian couples. I felt sorry for all of us.

I sought to insert myself in whatever places were possible, and, as luck would have it, Dewey and I carved out a little niche in the middle of the night that was just ours. It grew out of reward for finding the singular means (even if momentary) for solace during those long jags of inexplicable crying that grown-ups will attempt anything to soothe. There were things I already knew and things that Dewey taught me that often proved magical. They were those tricks—those private quirky maneuvers and quiet-of-night intimacies that cannot be found in manuals but that become the source of rituals that parents and babies share.

As Dewey and I grew our repertoire of songs, voices, expressions, holding patterns, and personal, private collaborative behaviors, I remember feeling bereft when others replicated them. The absorption of my hard-earned skills and techniques, and the forays by others into the little moments Dewey and I were learning to share, felt like trespassing, like theft of my connections. I felt I'd had to work so hard for them. If I couldn't share in the other magic, I wanted to create and hold onto my own. Dewey and I did create our own magic together. Over time we found our stride.

After the first several months our family underwent a drastic life-plan change. Margie's company sought to transfer her from our home and birthplace in New Jersey to Chicago. There was never guaranteed job security from one year to the next for me, as I worked in a grant-funded program, and both the ending of grant money and the deadline for Margie's employment coincided on June 30. We had little recourse but to leave the community of family and friends we had so carefully constructed and nurtured for ourselves and our children. So we heartbreakingly set ourselves and our things down in Oak Park, Ill., and fumbled through rebuilding our life. I became the stay-at-home mom—something I had never intended nor wished for—while Margie's responsibility and pressure at work grew exponentially. Margie and I struggled as we each resented what the other had. She would have given the world to be home with Dewey, and I would have given the same to find adult company and professional fulfillment at work. The complexity of these issues challenged us and our relationship in many ways.

The day-in-and-day-outness of Dewey's and my relationship mined for us many shared behaviors, routines, memories, and habits common to children and their most present parent. We often behaved in unison, and there was no mistaking that she was *my daughter* in almost every way. We looked nothing at all alike, but her expressions, her demeanor, and—once she began to speak—the patter of her words were like listening to a little Aimee. These are the fragments of magic that, combined, illustrated the connections so undeniable, so inexplicable, and so miraculous that we came to know and believe that love does make a family.

Still, when Margie was around there were these heart-wrenching moments when Dewey returned to her for comfort, which I felt fully equipped—but clearly uninvited—to supply. This was most often evident in those moments of total disintegration on Dewey's part. She sought refuge in Margie's breast. Once I was able to see past my puzzled resentment (after all, we managed fine when we were home alone together, and I felt confident that her every need was met in my care) I came to see that I could never replicate what Dewey found there. It was a history of which I was never a part, all of the predictable life-giving and sustaining ways of being that Dewey could only retrieve, even if momentarily, in the breast of Margie. These were the things that sustained and integrated her in ways that felt irreplaceable.

I know these feelings. I have found them in others, and I remember them in the breast of my own mother, and have missed them in the moments in my life when I've felt least integrated and most unable to retrieve and be fully rooted in my center. They come from the quietness of being, in a way that words and songs and rituals do not replace but will suffice—and even grow meaning all their own. Evolving from my initial assumption that all mothers are *equal*, what I came to know is that all mothers are indeed mothers, but—joyously— fundamentally not the same. The fruits of our differences create fertile ground from which we cultivate and nurture the richness of our families.

What I came to know is that there *is* a difference in the relationship between the biological mother and child and the nonbiological mother and child. And yet there are so few shared voices giving words to this painfully provocative experience. This silence felt deafening to me, and I realize that, as I did as a child, I dutifully obeyed the power of the silence by not speaking this truth. To deny this is to hurt ourselves in ways that cannot be healed. We *can* make the choice to celebrate the power of womanhood and the organic order of life while rejoicing in the endless potential for relationship borne out of connection and created out of commitment, developed and shared history, passion, caring, joy, belonging, and the total sense of saturation of our love—the love that makes us family.

I Hope the Blood Never Washes Off Your Hands: Transgender Parenting Crossing the Lines
by Loree Cook-Daniels

"I heard about your situation the night of June 1, 1999. I can honestly say that I had thought I had heard it all until I heard of your pregnancy. What a thing to do to your brothers. In an ideal world your actions would reflect on no one but yourself. In this world your actions will have consequences for the rest of the FTM population. Have you thought about what those consequences might be? Has it entered into your mind at all that you could be directly responsible for the death of another FTM, or two, or more? If you want to be a martyr for individualism and gender-bending at its strangest, by all means, go forth and bend. It is impossible for you to do that, however, since you're pregnant and still saying you are FTM. (I personally think that you tore up your FTM Club member card when this ill-conceived idea became a reality.) The media attention on you WILL get an FTM killed. I guarantee it. You WILL be responsible for a fellow FTM's death. I hope the blood never washes off your hands...." [1] —excerpt from an "open letter" by one FTM to and about another FTM

To be a transgendered parent is to walk a minefield daily. Everyone—and I mean everyone, including other transgendered persons as well as family members, friends, court officials, and casual observers—is a potential source of hostility, incredulity, and condescension. It's a life where you can simultaneously be completely invisible and terribly, terribly threatening; totally "ordinary" and thoroughly "bizarre." It's parenting the way lesbians and gay men parented 20 or 30 years ago—largely without useful maps and role models—but with some unique additional challenges.

Becoming a Transgendered Parent

"I do have friends that have had children before they were diagnosed as being [transsexual]...and I can understand such situations...[but] it seems so foreign to most of us, gay and straight alike, that anyone with true gender dysphoria would put themselves intentionally in a 'family way' after we have realized we are men..." [2]
—excerpt from a posting by an FTM on an America Online bulletin board

Remember the days when we had to explain how lesbians could possibly be mothers? Those days aren't past for transgendered parents. We are still explaining who we are and how in the world we came to have children.

First, who we are. Transgendered parents come in many flavors.[3] Many of us are transsexual, which can be broadly defined as persons who now live full-time in a gender role other than the one assigned at birth. Generally, transsexuals can be divided into one of two groups: male-to-females (MTFs) or female-to-males (FTMs). We may, or may not, use hormones to bring our body's appearance more in line with our social role, and may or may not have had surgeries to alter sexual characteristics. Officialdom may or may not recognize a gender and name we claim as ours.

The category of "transgender(ed)" may or may not include transsexuals; it does when I use it. For me, the term also refers to all who cross or blur gender roles, either on a full-time or part-time basis. It includes persons who sometimes present as male, sometimes as female; cross-dressers; inter-sexed persons (those formerly described as "hermaphro-dites"); and "two-spirit" persons. Butch lesbians and very effeminate gay men are sometimes included in the transgen-der category.[4]

I maintain that the category of "transgendered parents" also includes persons who (usually) aren't actually ourselves trans-sexual or transgendered. We are, however, partnered with transgendered parents and so must cope with whatever assumptions are made about our partners, children, and fam-ilies. I fall into this category: I am a nontransgendered woman married to an FTM man. My partner, Marcelle, conceived and gave birth to our son Kai while he was still living as a butch woman.

"How is Kai going to be able to handle Marcelle's change from his 'mommy' to his 'daddy'?"
—question posed to me by a straight friend when Kai was less than a year old

How we come to have children, not surprisingly, varies. Like lesbian and gay-male parents, many of us conceived or adopt-ed children in heterosexual partnerships before we "came out" or acted on our transgender feelings. With the growth in les-bian parenting has come an increase in the number of FTMs who, pretransition[5], became parents with another lesbian either through alternative insemination of themselves or their partner, or by adoption. Posttransition transgendered persons become parents through their partners giving birth, through adoption, or by partnering with someone who already has one or more children. In a few cases these posttransition children are biologically related to the transgendered parent, usually because the MTF had the foresight and resources to freeze her sperm before she transitioned. Situations such as the one that opened this essay—in which an FTM gets pregnant or an MTF succeeds in impregnating her partner "the old-fashioned way"—are fairly rare, both because hormones can affect fertility and because transsexuals are not immune to the social myths that "real men" don't get pregnant and "real women" don't beget children.

Fighting for Our Right to Parent

"It seems my little world has fallen apart here. My S.O.'s father has dumped some stuff on us. [He says it is] wrong for her to raise [our child] in this environment, that he [is] going to do anything that he [can] to get me outta her life, that he [is] going to pursue the court thing."

—MTF describing her father-in-law's reaction to the news of her transitioning

Once we have kids, we don't always get to keep them. In part because of transphobia and homophobia (and, in some cases involving lesbian- or gay-identified partners, heterophobia), many transgendered persons find that they must make a choice between their gender identity and preserving an intact family for their children.[6] Heterosexual as well as lesbian or gay partners often feel threatened by the idea of their partner changing genders. One researcher wrote, "There are feelings of betrayal, abandonment, and hostility of the nontranssexual parent. Many are so enraged at the transsexual parent that they defiantly oppose any contact with the child."[7]

If a heterosexual marriage involving a transgendered person breaks up and the nontransgendered parent seeks custody, he or she will find the courts extremely willing to indulge anti-transgender and antigay prejudices; typically, transsexual parents forced to go to court over custody or even visitation lose their cases. One of the reasons we lose is that, unlike lesbians and gay men, we have virtually *no* studies and *no* experts that testify to our ability to successfully parent children. Another reason we lose is because we don't have the financial resources to fight lengthy court battles. Being a transsexual can be expensive; there are the monthly costs of hormones, and surgeries can cost upwards of $50,000 (and are almost never covered by health insurance). Frequently, transsexuals end up downwardly mobile, as they change jobs to avoid the hassles and dangers of transitioning on the job, or get fired (since there are almost no laws forbidding employment discrimination against transgendered persons). MTFs often learn the hard way that women are often paid less even with *exactly* the same credentials.

"The first several years of counseling I had were directed at answering the problem my personal dilemma posed: How can I minimize the negative impact of my gender conflict on my kids? In other words, how can I save myself without sacrificing my own children in the process? Would it be best to just succumb to the long, painful death in which I was already dying from the inside out? Would it be possible to transition without causing my kids psychological harm? What is my best decision as a parent?

—MTF describing her initial struggles to deal with her transsexuality

Emotionally, transgendered persons may not be able to cope with everything involved in transitioning *and* rally the reserves necessary to fight for their kids. They also may not even realize they *should* fight for their kids; many transsexuals are told by other transsexuals that the only way they can be true to themselves is to completely abandon their old life, including their children, and start from scratch somewhere else.[8] They may also have internalized transphobia and believe that "queers" should not be around children.

Ex-spouses in cases where children were conceived or adopted *post*transition have also banked on judicial transphobia and homophobia. In one recent California case a woman tried to prevent her ex-husband from having contact with their daughter by alleging that she did not know her husband was an FTM when they married. Although the child had been conceived by alternative insemination using her husband's brother's sperm, the man was legally the father due to a presumption that all children born to a wife are the husband's. Had the woman succeeded in proving that her marriage was fraudulent from the beginning (i.e., that her ex-husband had convinced her to marry him under false pretenses), he would have lost his legal standing as a parent. Fortunately, in this case the court ruled in favor of the child having contact with both parents. Unfortunately, the outcome in this case is an anomaly; decisions ruling in favor of the transgendered parent are rare.[9]

Angry former spouses are not the only threat to a transgendered parent's contact with her or his children. Family members often threaten or attempt to keep children away from a transgendered parent as well. The wealthy parents of one MTF were so upset with her that they helped support her ex-wife and vowed that the MTF would "never get custody." So far they've succeeded: The judge won't even allow the MTF's children to visit her home—they meet in hotels.

Save Our Children

"My current challenge [as a parent] is getting a parent of my daughter's friend K to ALLOW K to go out in public with me."
—MTF explaining how transphobia affects her daughter's friendship with "K"

As any lesbian or gay-male parent can tell you, many people

still believe that lesbians and gay men pose threats to kids. Amazingly, however, transgendered people are apparently even *more* dangerous. Even though the "Love Makes a Family" photograph and essay display of lesbian- and gay-male–headed families has engendered huge controversies throughout the country, it was the inclusion of two *transgendered* families that initially freaked out the publisher who wanted to turn the display into a book. The publisher worried that *we* were going to be the reason schools gave for not allowing the book past their doors!

Even those who support our families are concerned about how we may endanger our children. The court employee investigating my petition to adopt Kai worried endlessly about the teasing he might endure as a result of having a transgendered parent. A four-page letter from us outlining the strategies we are using to prepare him for such inevitabilities (along with the videos of FTMs and lesbian or gay parents we sent him) helped reassure him that he was not contributing to the destruction of an innocent child. But even in his new role as our advocate, he insisted that we erase Marcelle's name from the "mother" slot on Kai's birth certificate. When we asked why, he told us that Kai should never have to reveal his parents' status and suggested that Kai might at some point need a security clearance. We bit our tongues rather than point out what was to us obvious: given how out we are nationally, it would be an act of self-sabotage on Kai's part to try to hide who we are. We also kept mum about the mind-boggling irony of the timing of the investigator's recommendation: The week this officer of the court was sitting in our living room telling us to teach Kai to lie, the country was in an uproar over the brand-new revelation that President Clinton had lied about his affair with Monica Lewinsky.

"I have seen the impact on children who were raised [without] a mother. I have no idea what impact it will have to reveal

to a child that 'Yes...you have a mother.... But your mother isn't your mother.... [Your] mother is your father....' "
—FTM professor of child psychology and counseling concerned about the psychological well-being of children birthed by FTMs

A more pressing concern for many people is how to "explain" sex changes to children. Even very sophisticated professionals are stymied by this "problem." I once had a lesbian therapist worry aloud that having our four-year-old children play together might be problematic. "I'm not ready to explain sex changes to my daughter," she said. Neither are many transgendered parents, it seems; one of the most common inquiries on the transgendered parents' E-mail support group I belong to is, "Exactly how do I explain it to the kids? Won't they be forever confused? Should I say anything at all?"

The truth is, young kids have no trouble at all accepting sex changes. Young children believe in the tooth fairy and Ronald McDonald; they see no reason to question the simple statement that someone they know as a man is becoming a woman. Older children, on the other hand, have been repeatedly told, "Once a girl, always a girl." Understandably, they sometimes have a harder time accepting the news that biology is *not* destiny. As with any such topic, conversations about sex changes should be led by the child's questions and intellectual level.[10]

The children who seem to have the most trouble are adolescents with a parent who is changing from their "same" sex to their "opposite." But even these teenagers, like the teenagers of newly out lesbians and gay men, usually come around with enough time and steadfast love. No, these concerns about the children are all projections; it's *always* the *adults* who have a hard time wrapping their minds around sex changes.

Recently I repeated to a MTF grandmother a conversation

I'd had with my five-year-old son, who has several times said he wants to be a girl: "I told him boys usually have penises and girls usually have vulvas. Since he has a penis, we *think* he's a boy, but we might turn out to be wrong."

"Oh, my God," my friend exclaimed, "You're going to confuse the hell out of him!"

I was left to wonder exactly who is confused: the woman with a penis I was speaking to, or my son, who knows that his daddy is a man who has a vulva and gave birth to him? Or is it me, who believes kids can—and should—understand the truth?

To Be or Not to Be: Invisibility

"I want to tell you that when you and Marcelle walked into the trans conference that Saturday morning with Kai, I had no idea who you were. That may not sound significant since we'd never met before, but to me it was rather phenomenal—once I realized you were Loree—because I had been reading all your messages on the PFLAG lists about Marcelle's transition and your adoption of Kai, and thought your story was so compelling and your energy and activism so inspiring. In other words, I thought I knew all about you and your family. Yet when I was in the same room with all of you, you managed to look so much like an "ordinary" male-female couple with child that I assumed you were all dedicated allies who had shown up to support someone else!

—comments from a colleague who, prior to the conference, knew me only through E-mail

As any queer can tell you, invisibility can be both a blessing and a curse. My family looks heterosexual. I'm positive that fact had a bearing on the success of my petition to adopt our son. First, it allowed me to petition under the less stringent "stepparent" rules, which I argued fit me because I was now legally married to one of my son's biological parents. Second, it appeared to impress our court investigator, who absolutely insisted that we permit his report to read that we are a "normal heterosexual family."[11]

Some families like this invisibility. A primary goal of many transsexuals is to "blend in," to become indistinguishable from those who have never questioned their gender. Indeed, some transsexuals have never revealed their gender past to their children.[12] Recently, a researcher trying to capture the oral histories of the oldest transsexuals tracked down an MTF believed to be one of the first individuals to undergo a full surgical sex change. But she refused to participate in the project because she didn't want to risk her (grown) children and grandchildren finding out that she's a transsexual.

"We are having parenting issues come up around invisibility. No books. Heather Has Two Mommies *doesn't work for us anymore, and there is no book called* Cindy Has a Dyke Mom and a FTM Dad. *We want her to understand that our family is different from lots of others, but it doesn't look like it on the surface."*

—lesbian partner of a FTM, commenting on her parenting struggles

Those of us who have a "queer" identity often chafe under this cloak of invisibility. Kai is not shy about telling others his father bore him. The problem is that many people don't believe him. We have always informed his day care providers and teachers that he is, in fact, telling the truth and that we expect them to respect that. But his young friends are a different story. We haven't figured out what to do about the neighbors, who come from a family that seems to adhere to rather strict gender rules. So far, we've just stayed out of the "My daddy did *too* have me!" arguments we overhear.

The price of trying to erase the invisibility of transgendered families, on the other hand, can be huge. Recently we were contacted by FTMs who wanted us to work with a Fox TV network producer on a documentary about FTMs. When the producer contacted us, he let slip a fact that had been unknown to the other men: The documentary was titled *Bizarre World*. When we expressed concern about the title, he sought to reassure us: "I would like to punctuate, though the title is sensationalistic, our mandate is to deliver a show that documents the strikingly odd of the human condition." We passed.

"On the up side, there is no longer the concerns about my gender. Seems that is accepted finally....Now we seem to be moving into the realms of lesbian concerns. And this seems to terrify [my wife's] mom, [my son's] grandmother. She is very concerned about [my son] being picked on because he lives with two lesbians."
—transitioning MTF's comments on the progression of her in-laws' concerns

Of course, "invisibility" is relative. My family is invisible because we seem to fit the heterosexual norm. Families that started out looking heterosexual will, if they stay together through transition, end up looking lesbian or gay male.[13] Children in these families have to deal not only with their parent's gender change, but also with homophobia. Either issue can prove to be the most difficult: In contrast to the mother-in-law referenced above, one college-age daughter complained that it would be far easier for her to explain that her parent was gay than that her parent is an MTF—at least her friends know about gays.

Finding Supportive Community
The hottest recent controversy by far in the FTM community was sparked when an FTM learned that a well-known FTM was not only pregnant, but also had spoken to a TV

crew during the pregnancy. The first man posted a scathing "open letter" on his Web site and reposted it on a public message board on America Online that quickly gathered attention. Although the pregnant FTM had his supporters, many of those who posted were livid at this man's "self-serving, self-aggrandizing" act. The outrage focused on several issues:

- Letting the general public know that some FTMs still have—and sometimes use—"female" reproductive organs might lead people to further disparage and perhaps even kill FTMs.
- Surgeons might refuse to perform hysterectomies on FTMs because of this man, arguing that he proves they might later change their minds and want children.
- An FTM's previous hormone use might pose a health hazard to his fetus.
- Some critics warn, "You're dooming a child to a life of freakdom."

Among the other choice public tirades (including, of course, the one that opened this essay) leveled at this man and his family by other FTMs were these gems: "Legally, everyone may have reproductive rights...morally, everyone should not be allowed to exercise those rights." "This is going to set us back 50 years." "When my wife and I have a child I will use...you as an example of an out-and-out freak."

When I asked my transgendered parents E-mail support group whether this type of parent bashing ever occurred within the MTF community, one respondent sent me this:

"When I told some members of the M to F community that I was holding off on hormones until [child] number 2 was born, most understood, but I also took some vitriol from those who had the attitude that I was: (A) crazy, since it is a foregone con-

clusion that [the] child [of a transsexual] would never have a normal life or (B) not genuinely a [transsexual] if I was willing to forgo such an important step as [hormone therapy] for, in effect, something as unimportant as a child."

There's often a comprehension gulf between parents and nonparents, so perhaps it's not surprising that childless transgendered persons don't always understand the lengths to which people will go to parent. But lesbian and gay-male parents would understand the desire to have children and the need to be supported in that endeavor, right? Well, maybe. Even there, we transgendered parents often have to buy a clue or two for our hoped-for allies. When I asked the leader of a lesbian/gay parenting group with more than 300 member families whether his group welcomed transgendered parents, he wasn't sure:

"My feeling is that we have a very open and welcoming group of families who, for the most part, treat people as they wish to be treated. However...most of us have little or no experience with transgendered folks, and that probably is a problem initially to many folks.... My advice to you is to try and find out. You probably won't connect with everyone, but you will make contact with a few friends, and what more can you ask for, eh?"

Hoping to get in on the ground floor of a program that *would* welcome my family, I volunteered to help a well-established queer organization develop their family program. After several rounds of discussions about what was needed and what I was hoping for, I was stunned to hear that the organization had made a preliminary decision to develop two separate support groups: one for lesbian and gay parents, and one for transgendered parents. "Uh," I said, "are you suggesting that I go to one group and my partner go to another?" They quickly backed down, but the message had already come through loud and clear yet again. Transgendered parents are threatening, invisible, and controversial because—by our very existence—we step on and over *everyone's* favorite lines.

> *"I agree that we all have our lives to live as we see fit...but where do we draw the line?... Do we have a responsibility to anyone except ourselves?... Should someone make the choice to give birth to a child when the risks to that child are potentially great? Should someone make the choice to give public notice of their highly divergent behavior when the risks to others, who may be seen as like them, are potentially great?"*
> —FTM commenting publicly on another FTM's pregnancy

I continue to proclaim that neither I, my family, nor other transgendered families (out or closeted) are a threat to each other or to anyone else in any other community. But I do so knowing that there are those within my own communities who believe that my simple act of public proclamation may well make me an accessory to murder.

1. Excerpt from an open letter from one female-to-male (FTM) transsexual to another, posted approximately June 3, 1999, on a Web site that has since been moved to http://www.landho.dreamhost.com/home.htm.

2. Unless otherwise noted, every quotation in this essay is from an E-mail. To protect both the innocent and the guilty I am keeping all quotations anonymous. Those relating to the pregnant FTM, however, were all posted on publicly accessible AOL "message boards" in early June 1999. All quotations related to that controversy that I've used in this essay were written by men I know to be FTM. Other quotations come from E-mails sent to me personally or to a transgender parenting E-mail support list in which I participate.

3. All these definitions are the author's alone; all terms currently associated with transsexual and transgendered persons are very much contested and

in flux. There is no consensus within the community about what terms should be used for which "kind" of persons.

4. Unfortunately, I do not have much experience with bigendered, cross-dressing, or intersexed parents. By default, then, most of the observations and examples used in this essay relate to transsexual parents.

5. "Transition" is the term used to designate the period and/or process during which an individual stops living in one gender role and begins living in another.

6. It is far too simplistic to say that transphobia, homophobia, or heterophobia is the sole cause of all family breakups involving transgendered persons. For a brief look at just some of the challenges involved see the article "Trans-Positioned" at http://www. members.aol.com/marcel-lecd/Transpositioned.html.

7. Green, R. "Transsexuals' Children." In *The International Journal of Transgenderism,* Vol. II, No. 4 (October-December 1998). http://www.symposion.com/ijt/ijtc0601.html.

8. It is crucial to note that it's not just transsexuals who are to blame for this "abandon everything" prescription. It was not that many years ago that professionals who "treated" transsexuals *required* them to abandon their families (or at least divorce their spouses) before they would grant permission for the transsexual to obtain hormones and/or surgery. Indeed, there are still sporadic reports of professionals requiring or at least advising their clients to abandon their families.

9. For a brief review of the legal status of transsexual persons (including some case citations) see the National Center on Lesbian Rights' briefing paper, "Representing Transsexual Clients: An Overview of Selected Legal Issues" (undated).

10. At this writing my son is five. Not surprisingly, we have had many conver-

sations about gender and sex changes, each building on the last as new questions occur to him. In the most recent he actually asked how doctors help a boy to become a girl, which led into a discussion of genital surgery. Many children will never pursue the topic this far. I also want to note that to help inoculate him against disbelief and outrage we have repeatedly told him that while some boys have vulvas and some girls have penises, "not everyone knows that."

11. We continue to be ambivalent about having finally acquiesced to this description. Ultimately, however, two arguments persuaded us: It was a relatively small principle to sell in exchange for our son's legal protection, and it amused us to think that the court investigator's definition of "a normal heterosexual family" includes one in which Dad birthed the child and Mom is a lesbian activist.

12. An excellent work of fiction that deals in part with the reactions of a child who doesn't learn that his father was an FTM until after his death is *Trumpet* by Jackie Kay (Pantheon Books, 1998).

13. Many transsexuals and/or their partners do identify as lesbian or gay male; others do not accept that identity, appearances notwithstanding.

The State of the State of
Queer Parenting at the Millennium
by Jenifer Firestone

This "State of the State" seeks to provide an overview of the major issues involved in queer parenting as it stands today, as well as the considerations LGBT parents and prospective parents face in the immediate future.

This overview is based on my ten years of counseling and educating LGBTs and mainstream institutions about the emotional, logistical, medical, and legal ramifications of alternative conception and parenting arrangements. While my experience has been situated within the evolving LGBT parenting scene in and around New England, it is important and instructive to be aware of the distinct issues concerning LGBT parenting experienced by people outside the few places where existing services are located. Likewise, LGBT men and women in New England have undergone distinct evolutions in the queer-parenting movement. At present the number of lesbians raising children and the number of attendant organizational developments, including the availability of and greater access to support services, is greater than that of and for gay men in our communities.

A 1998 *University of Illinois Law Review* article (No. 235, p. 339) reports that there are between 1 and 5 million lesbian mothers, 1 to 3 million gay fathers, and 6 to 14 million children of LGBT parents in the U.S. The San Diego–based Family Pride Coalition lists more than 160 LGBT parenting groups in 37 states across the U.S. and more than 20 worldwide, with new local groups being discovered all the time.

LGBT parenting groups have on their respective mailing lists more than 1,100 LGBT parents and prospective parents in Boston, 1,500 in Minnesota; 2,500 in New York City; and 400 in Chicago. We can also assume that there are thousands of LGBT parents who are not on any organized mailing list.

Gay-straight alliances exist in high schools in 35 states and in one-third of all public high schools in Massachusetts. There are 90 GLSEN (Gay Lesbian Straight Education Network) chapters nationwide as well as several national organizations advocating for the rights and fair treatment of LGBT parents and our children. Some of these include NCLR (National Center for Lesbian Rights); GLAD (Gay and Lesbian Advocates and Defenders); Lambda Legal Defense and Education; Family Pride Coalition, COLAGE (Children of Lesbians and Gays Everywhere); and Second Generation, a group for LGBT kids of LGBT parents.

Furthermore, an increasing number of adoption agencies and fertility clinics willing to work with LGBT prospective parents have made parenting substantially more accessible than it was 15 years ago.

All of this illustrates the tremendous increase within American society in our prevalence and organization, which has improved our families' social support and our ability to address homophobia in our communities. But complacence at this point in our evolution would be a big mistake, as racism, the daily struggles of poor and working-class parents, and homophobia continue unabated. Even though there are two LGBT parents groups in Virginia, a state judge took Sharon Bottoms's child away from her because she is a lesbian. Even in "The People's Republic of Cambridge" (Massachusetts), a huge uproar accompanied plans to bring the "Love Makes a Family: Living in Lesbian and Gay Families" photo-and-text exhibit to a local elementary school. And even in our own community the integrity of our families is compromised as increasing numbers of biological mothers deny the parentage of their nonbiological comothers when the couple breaks up.

White middle-class and upper middle-class LGBT parents and prospective parents predominate most organized groups, events, and programs for LGBT parents. This segregation should not obscure the realities of millions of poor, working-class, and LGBT parents of color. Lack of access to existing services and uneven resources to develop those that are needed is the very framework in which LGBT people are becoming parents.

As the saying goes, A mother's (or father's) work is never done. Progress is the process, not its completion. Being an LGBT parent in a major metropolitan area is not unrelated to making parenting an option for LGBTs in smaller cities and towns. And the tasks of raising our own children is inseparable from our responsibility to create communities in which being the child of LGBT parents is not a burden, but a birthright worthy of pride.

Rather than serving as a definitive report, this overview, I hope, will evoke a richer dialogue as LGBT parents and prospective parents around the country consider their experiences and visions in their own communities and relationships.

Queer Family Constellations: Traditional and Nontraditional Alternative Families

Since the beginning of the lesbian baby boom, one thing that has not changed is the same-sex version of the nuclear family as the most common model for LGBT-headed families with children. The majority of lesbian couples get pregnant using sperm from an anonymous donor via a sperm bank, and a smaller number adopt by choice or due to infertility problems, often related to age. Some lesbians have biological children with a man they know so that the child can know their biological father. Generally, the man has little to no regular involvement with or parental rights to the child. Some men do have regular involvement with the child, but the mom(s) is (are) almost always the primary parent(s). A very small number of lesbians actually share parenting responsibilities with their child's biological father(s).

Most gay male couples adopt their children. A much smaller but increasing number of gay men employ a surrogate mother, independently or through a professional agency, to bear them a child. Occasionally the surrogate is a family member or friend, but she relinquishes all parental rights, generally. A smaller number of gay men have children with a woman or women they know, with varying levels of involvement on the biological mother's part. Far more men than women are interested in sharing some level of parental involvement, but few women are comfortable sharing parenting rights and responsibilities outside their spousal unit. Common to families in straight and LGBT communities is the invisibility of single parents.

A small but growing number of lesbians and gay men are having biological children together and raising them in the context of a wide variety of arrangements. The chart at the end of this essay illustrates a spectrum of parental or familial involvement levels assumed by men and women in these arrangements.

By being a part-time mom I've discovered that I could design a permanent parenting situation that would honor my profound desire to be a mom (and trepidation about becoming one). It has been the most liberating experience of my adult life. Knowing numerous families of lesbians and gay men who have had children together, with widely varying levels of involvement with the children, has reinforced my belief that there are all kinds of wonderful ways to put a family together, as long as each of the parties' visions are clear, explicit, and complementary. Obviously, there are several other crucial ingredients to successful family arrangements, including honoring each other's relationship (or lack thereof) with the child while recognizing the possibility that one of the parties could have a change of heart, mind, or circumstance that could alter the original plan. In these situations the parties must work together creatively to find ways to, at least partially, accommodate the change without disregarding the original plan.

This is very dicey stuff. Lesbians and gay men who have children together have odd, hybrid relationships from the start. Even in the case of donors who don't plan to be very involved, or lesbians and gay men who are close friends, attempting to conceive and, to whatever extent, be involved with children is an extremely intimate endeavor for people who have chosen not be intimate in any other ways.

The presence of one of my daughter's fathers in the hospital room while I was in the excruciating process of having a miscarriage was quite bizarre. But in some ways it was more bizarre that the other dad was not there witnessing the demise of what would have been his baby.

Are we friends? Are we family? Who are we to each other, especially given our obvious preference for people of our same gender? I refer to this nebulous groping for how to relate to each other as "relational bushwhacking." Obviously, few people are interested in engaging in this lifelong activity, and those who are must maintain an open mind and heart while navigating the vast gray area in which these relationships are evolving.

This process would be manageable if we never ran into conflicts. But nothing makes a parent more defensive than a possible threat or challenge involving their child, as when a mom(s) denies a donor access to the child(ren) or when a donor asserts more contact than the mom(s) want. In such situations mutual respect frays badly. Women might be inclined to believe that the men (donors) don't really matter to the child, while men often assert their importance and/or rights. I think the bottom lines for all LGBT family relationships are respect for the status quo of any child's relationship with their grown-ups.

Lesbians and gay men who conceive children together do so for the sake of fulfilling the child's need to know—and possibly have relationships with—both biological parents, and for the richness these bonds can bring to the act of parenting. But this fulfillment can only be achieved if the parties involved are:

- clear, explicit, and in agreement about their expectations of one another's personal, financial, and decision-making involvement (or lack thereof) with the child;
- respectful of each other's roles and expectations;
- committed to honoring the written agreement they make (which they have signed and had witnessed by their attorneys and several friends and family members); and
- willing to adapt to changes that are bound to arise when dealing with people they know, as opposed to anonymous sperm donors or birth mothers.

While the majority of these arrangements have been successful and worthwhile, some have been disastrous, and I am horrified at the cavalier approach taken by some men and women when considering these arrangements. Prospective parents and their friends must acknowledge the complexity and high-risk nature of these situations; talk to other LGBTs who have had children with a man or woman they know; seek legal and interpersonal counseling; and make a pact with one another, pledging that any conflict will be resolved by every means outside a conventional court of law.

The Myth of the Security and Functionality of the Two-Parent Nuclear Family

Coparenting continues to be a commitment most people make only with their same-sex spouse. I regret our stubborn allegiance to the only-spouses-can-coparent model. For one thing, limiting our vision to a two-parent nuclear model is not necessarily an optimal arrangement, particularly when both parents work full-time; don't have easy access to close family or friends who can readily take care of the children overnight or on weekends; and are struggling to keep up financially, socially, politically, sexually, or otherwise.

Certainly, most gay and straight parents raise their children this way, but it takes a tremendous toll on the parents individually and as a couple. Most parents are perpetually exhausted, feel frazzled and torn in a million directions, and have given up most of the involvements and pastimes they enjoyed prior to having kids. Most haven't had a night, Sunday morning, or weekend to themselves—much less a few days—since their children were born.

The Christian Coalition–type folks would have us believe this is the way parenting is supposed to be and that raising children requires total self-sacrifice. I, for one, don't believe we need to buy this hook, line, and sinker. If one shares some level of parenting with a trusted, respected person (or people) outside the spousal unit, one has built-in time off from parenting. How many parents would not relish this opportunity? How many children would not benefit from having an expanded number of consistent, reliable, familial grown-ups to love and care for them? I believe LGBT parents and prospective parents have minimized the importance (I would say necessity), legitimacy, and feasibility of parenting that has built-in child-free time or part-time parenting.

My own decision to conceive and raise my child with a gay male couple has been an intimate, personal, and political leap for which I've faced skepticism and criticism even from many of my peers. People were skeptical about the enormous risk I was taking by agreeing to share control of my child with the men, and critical of my refusal to be a full-time mother. "How can you do that to your baby? Don't you miss her?" The sanctity of the mother-child relationship is alive and well, even in the LGBT community. Gay dads face this reality all the time when they have and/or raise children without a woman.

Although there are other families in the country like ours, my daughter's dads and I do not personally know any other similar families. Obviously, sharing some level of parenting with a nonspouse is a lifelong commitment that we are unaccustomed to making. It is complicated, requiring genuine mutual respect, some level of shared values, and the willingness and ability to process, solve problems creatively, and trust. But it could be considerably less problematic than the necessary follow-through on that lifelong coparenting commitment if a spousal relationship falls apart.

Spousal relationships between straight couples only last about 50% of the time, and there is no reason to believe LGBT couples will fare better in the pursuit of "forever." There is great danger in our culture's stubborn refusal to view "forever" as a goal rather than an absolute and definitive outcome, and to accept the remote possibility that a romantic, sexual, spousal partnership could change to the point that one or both partners lose the desire to maintain it.

One problem is that couples planning to have children rarely, if ever, make any provisions for the eventuality of a breakup. Of the hundreds of thousands of existing parenting lesbian couples, only a tiny fraction create a written coparenting document that talks explicitly about how they intend to parent their child(ren) if they break up.

"Well," indignant wanna-be lesbian moms say, "straight

couples don't do that." Well, you're right, I say, but at least 50% of straight nuclear families are a mess. Enough of us are the damaged products of rancorous divorce and parental disappearance or abandonment to prove it. Therefore, we should not use their process, or lack thereof, as our standard.

Furthermore, even in cases of second-parent adoption, the probate court system hasn't a clue what to do with us, and in its absence we have no system whatsoever. We leave our children's future relationships with their parents up to total chaos, battles of will, manipulation, and overt abuses of power. What kind of examples are we setting?

When people depend on you, buying life insurance is a good idea. It does not represent a lack of will to live a long life or lack of faith that you will. Parents buy life insurance because we know that, goddess forbid, unforeseen tragedies can happen, and we want to provide for our children. To do anything less to assure continuity in our kids' relationships with the most important people in their lives is unconscionable.

As for my own oddball parenting arrangement, it has been a pleasure, a challenge, and incredibly satisfying in terms of the excruciatingly wonderful child we've created and the relatively sane and satisfying life I've been able to have even though I am a quasi-single mom who makes very little money, works uncontrollable hours, and battles a variety of emotional demons.

As for my situation—which involves men who prefer men and a woman who prefers women (and has a lot of issues with men)—it hasn't been a day at the beach. We've had to adjust to many aspects of each other's personalities, lifestyles, and parenting styles. But it is my understanding that this is generally the case with spousal coparents too.

I think that in the new millennium the lives of LGBT parents, our children, and our community would be enhanced greatly if prospective parents could:

- pry themselves away from the false sense of security

derived from the nuclear family model;

• open their imaginations to the infinite possibilities of alternative family and parenting models;

• take their parenting seriously and realistically enough to make firm commitments to explicit written donor and coparenting agreements that make clear to each other; to their families and friends; to their therapists, mediators, and judges; and, ultimately, to their children exactly what their plans and expectations of each other are; and

• seek from their community the support and creative problem-solving assistance needed to honor the parenting agreements we make to each other and our children.

A Tale of Two Parenting Communities:
Lesbian Moms and Gay Dads From Straight Marriages

In the early '80s most LGBT families were headed by parents who had children from a previous heterosexual marriage and who had subsequently come out. These families were sometimes joined by the new, same-sex partner of the biological parent. Between 1989 and 1992 between 25 and 40 organizations of Gay Fathers of Greater (fill in the city) proliferated across the country, dealing primarily with coming-out issues, divorce, being gay, and making the transition to being "weekend dads." Today there are only approximately 15 such groups nationwide, as more gay men are coming out earlier in their lives and fewer men are going through the circuitous process of marrying and having children before coming out.

Lesbian mothers have also been extricating themselves from straight marriages for a long while but have never organized themselves in the same way formerly married gay fathers have. In the '70s and '80s lesbian moms in or out of straight marriages generally gravitated toward the broader organized feminist women's and explicitly lesbian communities. Quite often their social and political needs were met in these con-

texts, but their identities and concerns as mothers went largely unrecognized. In those early days the only path to parenthood was through heterosexual relationship, which rendered
lesbian motherhood an irrelevant aberration to the larger
community of lesbians.

Today things are still difficult for this population. For one
thing, in many states custody disputes between straight and
gay parents continue to horrify and abound. In her 1999 *Gay
Community News* article, "The Limits of Visibility: Queer
Parenting Under Fire," Nancy Polikoff states that in the '90s,
as in the '70s, a court could conclude that a lesbian mother
was exposing her daughter "to a lifestyle that is neither legal
in this state, nor moral in the eyes of most of its citizens." She
concludes that "to the Alabama mother who lost custody of
her daughter last year, it is no consolation that lesbian moms
in California or Massachusetts do not face such judicial hostility." The District of Columbia is still the only place in the
country that prohibits the use of sexual orientation as a basis
for denying custody or visitation.

Another problem for coming-out moms is that there are
fewer grassroots lesbian and feminist groups for them to hook
into. For many moms in straight marriages, increasing urban
sprawl renders them somewhat isolated in the suburbs. The
challenge of finding and getting to such groups in the cities
can be prohibitive, particularly for women who are not yet out
to their families. And, unfortunately, the groups that exist are
not particularly welcoming to married or formerly married
women.

In my neck of the woods many lesbians from straight marriages find their way to the Cambridge Women's Center,
which holds coming-out meetings and general rap sessions
for women over 30. But out lesbians can't seem to see these
women as "real lesbians" worthy of lesbian friendships, or
sexual or romantic relationships. In general, never-married
lesbians still seem to be uninterested and unwilling to

appreciate the challenging complexities faced by mothers coming out in their 30s, 40s, and 50s to husbands, older children, and in-laws.

Finding common ground between lesbian moms from straight marriages and moms having children as out lesbians forces us all to stretch. As a general description, the former are in the throes of coming out; have older children; have been living heterosexual lives; have husbands or ex-husbands with whom they may or may not be battling for custody of their children; do not necessarily identify with a lesbian, feminist, or political orientation; and are sometimes influenced by internalized homophobia.

More often than not, this separates them from less straight-appearing lesbians who have been out for many years; have younger children; have been living single or partnered lesbian lives; can't imagine having a husband; do identify with some kind of organized lesbian/feminist political community; and are not terribly concerned with appearing straight.

While these generalizations do not apply to every mom in these respective categories, they are definitely operative elements that have kept these two groups of lesbian mothers almost entirely separate from one another. In the same ways that middle- and upper-class women should not turn their backs on women on welfare, never-married and out lesbians are in a position to bridge this unnecessary gap by being welcoming, interested, and supportive of the unique struggles of lesbian moms in or out of heterosexual marriages. This may seem passé, but I still believe that sisterhood is powerful. In this case, political activism takes the simple form of individuals being compassionate. There is no excuse not to participate.

Most of the Gay Fathers groups have never made any pretense of addressing issues of never-married, wanna-be, or new gay dads who are increasing in number. As a group facilitator, I couldn't wait to run separate groups for moms from straight marriages and lesbian moms who'd had kids after they were already out: The issues were so different that the women couldn't relate to or support one another. Concurrently, dwindling numbers have caused organizers of Gay Fathers of Greater Boston to consider expanding their focus to include new and wanna-be dads—which brings all LGBT parents to an interesting organizational crossroads. The time is here for the independent, sex-segregated organizations for gay fathers and lesbian moms to form unified, all-inclusive, local LGBT parent groups—with separate discussion/support groups and networks for specific subgroups of LGBT parents, and COLAGE groups for our kids. If we merged our mailing lists and newsletters, we could conserve our meager monetary and human resources and learn a little something about each other as well. This is not rocket science—and has certainly already been done in places such as Minnesota and San Diego.

Developmentally speaking, overcoming oppression has legitimately begun in the context of support and self-identification with one's particular oppressed group, and that context should be preserved for the steady stream of newcomers and old-timers. However, having achieved some personal sense of comfort, stability, and pride as a part of that particular group, we must be able to look around and turn some of our attention to related groups who are, in fact, our kin. Being able to see past differences is enriching and makes us infinitely stronger as a diverse network of LGBT families.

Many Options, Many Issues

As mentioned earlier, becoming a parent is much more feasible now than it was in the early '80s. Still, there is no cheap, easy, risk-free, or problem-free way for gay people to have children. If one conceives with an anonymous donor, one must do business with sperm banks and doctors, possibly facing the child's dissatisfaction with knowing a donor number instead of a dad. Conceiving with a man or woman one

knows can preclude involvement with medical establish-
ments and possibly include involvement with both biological
parents. For better or worse, it is accompanied by lifetime
involvement with the other biological parent, and the issues
and risks that entails. Adoption forces one to deal with invasive, expensive bureaucracies; to (sometimes) feign being
single and straight; and (frequently) to live with the issues of
being white parents raising kids of color and/or with special
needs. Paying a woman to bear and relinquish a child makes
surrogacy the most expensive and controversial route to parenting, but all options require considerable commitments of
time, emotional energy, and money.

In addition to the pros and cons specific to each of these
various options, all LGBT parents must face the heartache,
anxiety, and lack of control involved with all of them. No one
who tries to get pregnant knows if they will—or how long it
will take. At least two thirds of my clients have struggled with
infertility problems, including donors' and dads' low sperm
counts. The emotional roller coaster of repeated insemination
attempts can take an enormous toll. No matter how much
intervention we apply, we cannot control our bodies or the
adoption agencies who hold the key to our parenthood.

I understand prospective parents' preoccupation with the
nuts and bolts of adopting or conceiving children, but equally important are the issues and implications involved in each
option. The following overview of the various routes to parenting available to LGBTs today focuses on these common,
but rarely discussed, concerns.

Anonymous Donor Insemination

The Sperm Bank of California is a feminist, nonprofit
sperm bank that grew out of the Oakland Feminist Women's
Health Center in 1982. It was founded to provide lesbians
and single heterosexual women access to donor sperm
because mainstream providers were unwilling to inseminate

them. While the sperm bank itself is still in operation, they have stopped actually performing inseminations. In its January 1999 newsletter the bank announced, "Fortunately, in recent years the climate of fertility services has evolved, and there are many practitioners now available to support all our recipients in the process of donor insemination.... Over time, the DIP (Donor Insemination Program) became less relevant, until by late 1998 there were only seven recipients enrolled in this program."

Lesbians have had a tremendous impact on the evolution of the donor insemination industry by demanding that more information be available to recipients and their children about anonymous donors from sperm banks. In the early days of DI, users had little to no information about a donor, much less a choice about which donor they would use. Like adoption, DI was a vague and murky secret maintained to protect the identity of the biological father and assuage infertile fathers-to-be who wanted to minimize the significance of their missed biological connection to their children.

Lesbian mothers, on the other hand, planned to hide nothing from their DI-conceived children and wanted as much information as possible about donors. Today, in addition to the availability of detailed donor profiles (containing three-generation medical histories, handwritten essays, and more), there are two banks that allows the donor, at the child's request, to be identified to the child when s/he turns 18. Some banks offer audiocassettes or videotapes of the donor as well as photographs and essays. Since sperm banks now ship frozen specimens in portable tanks of liquid nitrogen vapor, women across the country have access to this basic technology.

They must, however, have a medical provider willing to authorize their access to the sperm bank. This patriarchal gatekeeping poses a challenge to lesbians in conservative communities where doctors are unwilling to help lesbians have children. Given that most lesbians can impregnate themselves without the assistance of a doctor, and given that no one has caused themselves bodily harm from a home insemination with sperm from a sperm bank, it is odd that doctors have ended up in the position of determining who can and cannot bear children.

The main issue with DI concerning anonymous donors today is the same as it was 15 years ago: How will it be for a child never to know her/his biological father? This concern has been repeatedly articulated by adoptees who don't want their struggles with closed adoption records to become the legacy of children of the lesbian baby boom.

In reality, most DI offspring have very little curiosity or concern about a biological father who is a nonentity in their lives. They say they don't miss having something they never had in the first place and that their two moms are all the parents they need. The fact that lesbian moms tell their children frankly, but age-appropriately, about the nature of their conception as soon as the child expresses an interest eliminates negative feelings that are borne of secrecy or that mislead the child. On the other hand, some children are almost obsessed with the daddy question from a very early age. The issue for lesbians considering anonymous donor insemination is that one cannot know in advance which way their child will feel. They must be prepared to explain to the child why they had them the way they did and help their child through whatever daddy-related feelings they may or may not have over the years.

This is another situation in which the separateness between men and women in many of our lives and communities is particularly problematic. While adult gay people may not have much interest in members of the opposite sex, their children very well might. Lesbians raising sons can attest to the fact that parenting is no place for separatism. Many lesbians and gay men have few local opposite-gender friends and relatives to enrich their children's lives. For this reason, we in Boston are starting an Aunts and Uncles Program to institutionalize a bridge to the LGBT gender gap. Interested LGBT nonparents will be matched up with kids of opposite-gender LGBT parents who would like an additional reliable adult in the child's life. Once again, our children could benefit greatly by their parents' abilities to expand their network beyond the bounds of personal gender preference.

Adoption

Adoption is more complicated. In 1998 nine hostile bills were introduced across the country to restrict gays and lesbians from adopting and becoming foster parents. Fortunately, none of these passed, and New Hampshire overturned their ban on gay adoption; Florida stands alone in their criminalization of gay people adopting. However, there is much upcoming legislation on the horizon to prohibit adoption and foster care by LGBTs, and Utah and Arkansas both passed regulations that institutionalize these prohibitions. Colorado, Wisconsin, and Connecticut denied second-parent adoptions to nonbiological lesbian mothers (NGLTF Policy Institute, 1998 Capitol Gains and Losses). In addition, Mississippi passed a bill in April 2000 that outlaws same-sex couple adoption.

While adoption by LGBTs is legal in almost every state, homophobia among certain social workers in adoption agencies can make it difficult. Since adoptions are facilitated on the state level, prospective parents must find an LGBT-friendly agency in their state and adopt as a straight single parent. Increasing numbers of adoptive parents have found agencies with which they could be out in their home studies, and some lesbian and gay couples have actually been able to adopt domestically as a couple.

But I find it maddening to constantly keep up with the capriciousness of adoption agencies that are fickle in their willingness to work with LGBTs. It will take deliberate and systematic outreach and education to increase the numbers of adoption agencies who are willing to work with LGBT prospective parents; who are knowledgeable about the crucial subtleties of writing up our home studies; and who are committed to being advocates for placing children with us.

As more LGBTs adopt, our families and communities also adopt the inherent issues and controversies associated with white parents raising children of color. Becoming a multicultural family in communities that are culturally segregated can be painful and challenging for kids as well as parents. Many white adoptive parents go to great lengths to ensure that they and their children are involved with other families with children from the same country or cultural background. But I know one parent who wept when her daughter cried about being the only brown-skinned child in her school. Some adoption workers would say that woman had no business raising her brown-skinned child in an all-white community.

A recent article in the journal *Social Work* (Vol. 44, No. 5, September 1999) revisits the reasons many black social workers oppose transracial adoption, which was most strongly asserted in the '70s. Despite the prevalence of transracial adoption in LGBT communities, providing for the development of transracially adopted children's healthy cultural identity and sense of self continues to be a major child rearing challenge.

Looking again to community to help provide what parents alone cannot, our Aunts and Uncles organizing committee intends for this program to support kids of color by providing them with adult companions of color—one small step in acknowledging, considering, and creatively addressing this difficult issue.

Assisted Reproduction

Because a substantial majority of out lesbians and gay men postpone childbearing until they are in their late 30s or early

40s, diminished fertility can be a major problem requiring medical intervention. While access to reproductive assistance has improved enormously, LGBTs from all over the U.S. and abroad come to a few major American cities, since willing providers are still not available in most places. Only a tiny handful of providers nationwide will inseminate a woman with sperm from a known but unrelated man, and the Food and Drug Administration seems hell-bent on making it even more impossible than it currently is for gay men to get their sperm tested and frozen. Where there are facilities willing to work with us, medical staff members' disdain for, discomfort around, or lack of familiarity with us is often evident in the care we receive.

The most inaccessible piece of reproductive technology is that of sperm washing for HIV-positive men who want to be biological fathers. This relatively simple and inexpensive process, which separates the sperm from the seminal fluid that contains white blood cells and HIV, has been used successfully in Italy for many years. But in the U.S. the paralyzing combination of liability paranoia and social stigma has kept it completely out of reach. Obviously, many people don't think HIV-positive people should become parents—although it is hard to tell if this opinion comes from concern for the children or is based on punitive sentiments about HIV-positive people, given the improved health and life spans of many people with HIV.

Considering the substantial number and influence of LGBT medical professionals throughout the country, it would seem LGBT parents and prospective parents could prevail upon GLMA (Gay and Lesbian Medical Association), Dyke Doctors, and related groups to develop and cultivate greater networks of professional referrals to improve gay people's access to DI and other assisted reproductive technologies.

On the other hand, I wonder about the extremes to which we take this technology. One older lesbian I know had embryos from anonymous egg and sperm donors implanted in her uterus so that she could give birth for a second time. Several lesbian couples have taken one of their eggs, had it fertilized in vitro, and then implanted it in the uterus of the other woman so that they could both be biological moms.

These stories illustrate our intense conflict over the importance of biology. Regarding adoption and the relationships between children and their nonbiological parents, we say biological connection is irrelevant. Yet we go to incredible lengths to create such a connection. I realize these are individual choices reflecting the parents' needs more than the children's, and I appreciate that in many parts of the country gay people have the right (if they have the means) to choose how they will become parents. The new assisted reproductive technologies, however, entail many health risks as well as psychological and financial costs that may not be fully appreciated by prospective parents.

Like most new drugs, the long-term side effects of fertility drugs are not definitively known, and the short-term side effects are tolerable and not experienced by everyone who uses them.[1]

I wonder, though, if women who undergo these high-tech procedures are in some level of denial about the risks involved in taking such heavy-duty drugs in order to have a biological connection to their child. Furthermore, I question why that biological connection is important enough to justify the risks. Women who elect to use high-tech assisted reproduction to attain a biological connection say that it will enable both moms to feel more emotionally connected to the baby, share more equally in the pregnancy, and be legitimately recognized by unsupportive family members or judges as "the real mom." Taking into account the extreme measures required by these contrived connections, it might be cheaper,[2] healthier, and far less invasive to engage in some dialogue about ways in which nonbiological moms have come to terms with "the real mom" issue. In her article, "This Child Does Have Two Mothers…" (*Georgetown Law Journal*, February 1990), Nancy Polikoff defines a parent as "anyone in a functional parental relationship that a legally recognized parent created, with the intent that an additional parent/child relationship exist." While medical acrobatics make biological connections possible, I think it behooves our community to look more closely at this definition and at what individual family members and friends can do to truly live by it.

Surrogacy

Gay men have benefited from access to reproductive technology as increasing numbers have looked to treatment for male infertility (much more common than most people think), egg donation, and traditional and gestational surrogacy[3] as their paths to biological fatherhood. In addition to LGBT-owned-and-operated surrogacy agencies in California and Massachusetts, there are several agencies in the Midwest that have worked with gay clients for years.

Surrogacy, however, remains the most controversial parenting option for gay as well as straight people. Many progressive providers and community members are disturbed by the built-in termination of the mother-child bond and/or are uncomfortable with the potential exploitation of women who would be surrogates.

So when clinical intervention is required, gay-identified surrogacy agencies must find reproductive technology specialists who are willing to assist gay men with surrogacy (though not necessarily comfortable doing so). In Boston our clients waited months for a local hospital to garner permission from its ethics committee to facilitate a gestational surrogacy arrangement with gay men. Even after permission was granted the task of familiarizing social workers of clinics, nurses, doctors, and managed-care personnel about gay families was just beginning. Our most allied doctor at the clinic was incredulous at the idea that a gay man's sister wanted to be an egg donor for her brother's partner. Of the numerous doctors at that clinic, only a few are willing to work with our gay clients. A gay doctor at that clinic is not among them.

In addition, surrogacy is a very strenuous way to have a child—emotionally, financially, logistically, and interpersonally. Such a pregnancy can involve one or two gay men, a surrogate (or gestational carrier), an egg donor, and their families, not to mention clinic staff. That involves a lot of people, schedules, feelings, perspectives, and personalities.

The dynamic gay men often bring to this mix is that they are, in general, racially and financially privileged, are accustomed to having a substantial amount of control over their lives, and are unaccustomed to having to consult with someone else to get what they want. By contrast, the surrogates (who have their issues as well) are generally working-class or poor.

Surrogacy presents one of those weird hybrid situations that is part business deal and part intimate, lifelong personal relationship. In my experience intended parents do not necessarily recognize the implications or power dynamics inherent in this situation. Even though I am excruciatingly aware of these dynamics, I have never felt particularly skilled in negotiating them.

I have also found problematic the fact that many well-off gay men are neither feminists nor conscious about the unpredictability (uncontrollability) of women's bodies, the extent to which surrogates themselves must cope with this confounding physiological defiance of men's determination. One gay couple instructed the surrogate to take Clomid (a fertility drug) after one unsuccessful insemination. They were outraged and tried to fire me when I told them and the surrogate that I thought the use of drugs after one cycle attempt was premature and that I was sure the doctor would say the same. It was as though the surrogate's body, as part of their universe, should do their bidding on their schedule, regardless of potential side effects on the woman's body or the fact that, as lesbians well know, getting pregnant can take time. Women's bodies are not their machines, even if they are paying $25,000 to $55,000 for the use of them.

I do not believe, as many people do, that surrogacy is inherently exploitative of women. On the contrary, most surrogates I've known are self-possessed, have had gratifying relationships with their IPs (intended parents, in surrogacy lingo), are clearly and positively motivated, and feel highly empowered by their surrogacy experience. But none of the parties involved in these arrangements can necessarily appreciate how stressful and lengthy the process can be, much less be able to handle the stress with a consistently peaceful or empathic countenance. Those of us who believe in surrogacy as a legitimate route to parenting must improve the process by infusing it with some kind of "Class, Gender, and Feminism 101." Having a sense of entitlement and indignation with a process that we know from the outset to be painfully intense and complicated is not helpful.

Legal Liabilities

Second-Parent Adoption

One of the giant leaps to equality for LGBT parents has been second-parent adoption, whereby a parent who is not related to a child biologically or through marriage but who shares child rearing responsibilities with the legal parent can legally co-adopt a child. This tool gives the nonbiological parent legal standing as a bona fide parent with standing to pursue shared custody of the child if the partners break up. Courts in 21 states have granted second-parent adoption at some level, but access to second-parent adoption varies state by state, county by county, and judge by judge. In Massachusetts, Vermont, New York, the District of Columbia, and New Jersey second-parent adoptions are available statewide. In Colorado, Connecticut, and Wisconsin such adoptions have been denied.

Second-parent adoption, however, is no panacea. In Massachusetts a divorcing biological mom denied custody and visitation to the nonbiological mom even though they had completed a second-parent adoption years before. The judge appointed a guardian *ad lietem* (GAL), an attorney ordered by the court to represent the child, to investigate the situation. Despite the adoption the GAL had no idea what to do with this family; possibly, he had never seen lesbians before. Ultimately, after years of legal battles, the nonbiological mom was granted only minimal visitation. When custody is challenged, some divorcing second parents are treated like the bad father in a heterosexual divorce, receiving inadequate visitation rather than joint custody, with the biological mom calling all the shots and clearly having the upper hand. Second-parent adoption gives LGBT parents the tool to ensure family continuity in cases of separation. But when we, for whom it was uniquely fashioned, toss it aside like some sort of liberal judicial misunderstanding, I'm afraid that judges, GALS, and social workers lack the resolve or familiarity with our families to truly honor the adoption itself.

Lesbian Custody Disputes and the Development of an LGBT Family Ethic

Unfortunately, the privatization of our family relationships, coupled with our individual inabilities to amicably resolve personal conflicts, is the greatest legal vulnerability LGBT families face, and it is self-imposed. While we have made enormous institutional strides in improving the lives of LGBT families, we remain abysmally unevolved at creatively and productively working through crises in our family relationships, particularly those between donors and recipients, and between divorcing biological and nonbiological moms.

In a three-month period of 1999 the National Center for

Lesbian Rights received 45 calls from nonbiological/nonlegal lesbian mothers who feared or were actually denied access to their children following a breakup with their lesbian partner. In the first nine months of 1999 the Family Pride Coalition received 72 calls from mothers involved in custody disputes with their lesbian ex-partners, compared to 45 calls from mothers disputing custody with their ex-husbands.

The incidence of these disputes is exacerbated by our community's perpetuation of the notion that family relationships are private and nobody else's business. This used to be the excuse for not intervening in incidents of child abuse and domestic violence. Lesbian custody disputes are the elephants in the gay parenting community's living rooms, and discussion about them has been essentially nonexistent. Neither our children or our communities at large are well-served by this taboo.

The Massachusetts and Colorado supreme courts ruled that some nonbiological moms are de facto parents with legal standing to pursue joint custody and visitation. A similar case is to be decided by the SJC in Rhode Island. However, Florida, California, and Wisconsin supreme courts have decided otherwise, wreaking havoc in the lives of hundreds of LGBT parents and their children.

We can't have it both ways. When we're in love with our partners, we want the world to treat us like a "real" family, but when we split up, we dismiss the rights and responsibility of the coparent. We're sending mixed messages to our children, to the straight world, and to ourselves about what constitutes a family and a "real" parent.

As we grow in number and take our rightful place among other families in our communities, LGBTs must develop and live by a community ethic of our own that says, regardless of whether the probate courts or anyone else acknowledges our relationships with each other as a couple or with our children, *we* honor those relationships. LGBT couples who choose to have children together need to recognize that parenting is a lifelong commitment you make *to the children*, regardless of the demise of the parents' relationship with each other. And we need family members, friends, lawyers, and concerned members of the community to assert this ethic and support divorcing couples to live by it. It is time to talk about the second-class status of nonbiological and nonadoptive parents, then address the power imbalance in real, practical, compassionate ways. "Protecting Families: Standards for Child Custody in Same-Sex Relationships" was created expressly for this reason. This document articulates ten behaviors or principles that constitute respect for our families by maintaining the children's parental relationships in times of crisis or breakup.

We need to establish our own customs that make sense for our unique families. We can arrange family/community ceremonies to welcome the new baby/child and publicly acknowledge and commit to her/his family constellation. We can publicly assure our children that, while life is full of changes, this carefully chosen family of parents, donor/dads, etc. will always be their family and that each family member will forever honor and appreciate that child's relationship with each of them.

We could make use of "godparents" or other individuals who are mutually trusted by all of the parents to witness the recognition of these family members, to hear why they chose each other, what they each felt the other(s) would bring to the child's life, and to step in and assist if problems threaten the relationships to which the child is accustomed.

At this critical point in our evolution we must recognize that the "alternative" nature of our families only *begins* with alternative ways of becoming parents. The viability of our individual families and our communities of families depends on our commitment to focus on alternative ways of conducting our family relationships; resolving our family disputes; and involving friends, family, and community members in the process.

Public Enemy Number 1: The Religious Right

They are huge, rich, well-organized—particularly on the state and local levels—and their members are incredibly active and action-oriented. They'd hate for LGBTs, our families, and our efforts and inroads to be accepted as first-class citizens of this country, both as part of the mainstream and as a community unto ourselves. They lead the pack in every federal, state, and local effort to prevent us from adopting or becoming foster parents to parentless children; to prevent second-parent adoptions and LGBT marriages; to block the creation of gay-straight alliances in high schools; and to undermine or obliterate any attempt to promote understanding and decency about gay people in schools so that LGBT kids and kids of LGBT parents can learn and grow in some semblance of safety.

They accuse us of having children to make a political statement. What a joke! With all the political statements yearning to be made, there are much easier ways to make them than having children. I have worked with hundreds of LGBT parents and prospective parents, and not one of them has wanted children for political reasons.

On the contrary, one member of a lesbian couple who was not in agreement about having a child said, "One of the reasons I don't want to have a baby is because I don't want to have to be some kind of militant lesbian activist!" I told her that while I didn't think she necessarily had to be militant (although I often have to restrain myself), I did think she would have to be an activist, which is what LGBT parents who advocate for our kids have to be. As Kevin Jennings, executive director of GLSEN, recently said, "In the end, what really matters in the lives of LGBT families is the second-grade teacher who is teaching their daughter/son." If that second-grade teacher isn't comfortable with and supportive of that child's family, doesn't know how to explain it appropriately to other children and their parents, or doesn't know how to make lessons more inclusive of family diversity, it is up to parental responsibility to help remedy what is otherwise a daily and untenable situation for the child. We need to gather the growing body of age-appropriate curriculum materials addressing LGBT issues and families, we need to make sure our kids' teachers and librarians have the guidance and support from school principals to use those resources, and we need school board members and superintendents to provide leadership in promoting zero tolerance for "isms"—including heterosexism—in our kids' schools.

Parents in every elementary school could arrange with the principal to devote one staff meeting each year to discussing teachers' concerns about addressing homophobia in their classrooms. They could show the eight-minute video *Both My Moms' Names Are Judy* or the short version of *It's Elementary* and talk about specific answers to children's questions that take religion and "morality" into consideration. Participation by a few parents in these meetings would serve to educate teachers and help them feel more confident dealing with these issues in their classrooms. Assured that their supervisors support them if more conservative parents object, educators and parents could transform the ethic of school communities over time. There are many other specific activities like this one in which individuals and groups of parents can engage.

Being out and being visible are the most effective, logical, and natural ways to provide teachers, students, parents, and administrators with the direct experience of real live gay people that is needed to counter the lies strategically promoted by the Christian right.

Dehumanizing a people by denigrating and destroying their families is an old and insidious tactic for destroying an entire people from the inside out. White society used this tactic against black people during slavery, and the Christian right is resorting to a "more civilized" version today. They are doing everything in their power to deny that we are real families and to make it difficult or impossible for us to function as families, then trash *us* for not having family values.

How dare they try to claim some corner on the market for human nurturing? Having a family is every person's birthright, and it is an outrage that the Christian right has appointed themselves the family police, determining who is and can have, or be, a family. The time for local LGBT parents and our allies to develop concrete strategies for addressing homophobia in our children's schools is long past due.

We don't have children to make political statements, but for better or worse, LGBTs' having children requires political action. We cannot bring kids into an unjust and homophobic world without taking action to ameliorate that injustice and homophobia, particularly as it is manifested in our children's worlds.

Conclusion: To Be or Not to Be Like Straight Families? We Have to Talk About It

Our Reluctance to Discuss Unique Aspects of Our Families That Straight People Use Against Us

A certain amount of tension has always existed among gay people: between those who insist "We're just like everybody else" and those with the sense that we are very, very different from straight people. Though most people's lives are a combination of both, the point where one falls on the "just like" versus "very different from" spectrum is a matter of personal inclination, sociopolitical identification, etc. However, bringing children onto the spectrum seriously complicates matters.

Our families indisputably differ in some ways from most straight families. The fact that our families generally involve a biological and a nonbiological parent of the same sex makes us very different from straight families. While LGBT parents' opinions about the significance of these characteristics differ, these characteristics are also some of the reasons straight people are uncomfortable with or make a case against our families.

My concern is that, in an effort to refute these differences or purported "weaknesses" in our families, we minimize their significance to the children and/or deny that these are issues at all. When I sent out a letter inviting nonbiological moms to a discussion about being nonbiological moms of children conceived by their partners, one parent wrote to me saying that my use of the terms *biological* and *nonbiological* was divisive and unnecessarily focused on the biological origins of the child. When I suggest that parents send their child to a COLAGE group, some parents say that their child has no need or interest in such a group.

Quite frankly, for many LGBT-headed families these issues never do come into play. Many biological and nonbiological moms are virtually indistinguishable to their children and to each other, particularly if they are able to equalize their legal status with second-parent adoption. Most gay men raising daughters experience few, if any, instances in which the absence of a mom presents major problems. But the legal nonbiological mom who cannot feed, comfort, or put her infant to bed because her baby will only nurse and refuses a bottle is often distraught. For the adopted son of two gay dads who was given up by his birth mom and so has two dads and no mom, the Mother's Day Tea at school is a devastating experience. The son of lesbian moms who really wants a man around has a legitimate desire. These are not defects in our families but important issues that arise, which we need to talk about and handle in creative and effective ways.

The problem with parents' defensiveness about hearing even a reference to these situations is that it automatically shuts down any discussion on the matter, isolating those who do have questions or concerns and depriving us all of learning about the broad range of experiences of families with a biological and a nonbiological mom, dads raising daughters without moms, etc. We shortchange ourselves and our families if we deny or ignore these unique aspects of LGBT families. I urge parenting groups to organize opportunities for LGBT parents, our kids, and prospective parents to discuss their personal experiences with these issues—good, bad, and neutral—in a supportive, nonjudgmental atmosphere. This kind of open exchange could reduce individual isolation and shame, expand our knowledge of the families we are creating, and improve our children's overall mental health and comfort level with the world we've brought them into.

Where Are the Words? No Wonder No One Understands Who We Are!

Another challenge in talking about our families is that we have such inadequate language. While we are referred to and often refer to ourselves as "alternative families," sometimes I don't think we are alternative enough. Why haven't we invented language that accurately describes our unique familial relationships? Gay men who donate sperm have done so in the context of various levels of involvement with their child(ren). Yet we still have only two words, *donor* and *dad*, and they do not reflect the actual relationship between the child and the man. Nor do they describe the relationship between the man and the women who used his sperm.

Don't we need more affirming words for ex-lovers, particularly when we continue to coparent our children and evolve those formerly romantic partnerships into amicable or loving family relationships? It's bad enough that we continue to stumble when referring to our "life partner/spouse/lover/boyfriend/girlfriend/significant other/domestic partner." The fact that we have only two words for non–blood-related relationships in general—*friends* and *lovers*—gives the impression that those are the only two possibilities when, in fact, there are infinite worthwhile variations.

The problem with such limited relationship language is that

it actually limits our thinking about the number and kinds of relationships that are possible and legitimate. Regardless of the actual relationship, it is difficult for a "donor," his child, or anyone who knows them to recognize the importance of their relationship when the only word to describe him is *donor*. If he is not a custodial dad but is more than a known donor with no ongoing involvement, doesn't he deserve a noun of his own?

At my daughter's naming ceremony my father was earnest and good-natured when he asked how he should introduce my daughter's two fathers to the 100-plus friends and relatives who assembled with the rabbi in my sister's backyard to witness our unusual family. "They're not my son-in-laws, are they?" Apologetically I could only reply, "No, Dad, they're not your son-in-laws. You can say they're Hannah's dads. But in terms of who they are to you or to me, we just don't have the words yet."

The computer industry has not been bashful about creating an entire vocabulary to describe their reality. Our community should fulfill its responsibility to provide our families with the necessary words to describe our reality. We should collectively call upon the linguists among us to have a field day. Having nouns to accurately describe who we are could assert the credibility our relationships deserve.

Making Community for Our Families: Raising Our Kids in the Burbs, Boonies, or LGBT Ghettos?

Another issue that may or may not set us apart from heterosexual families involves the significance of where we live. As I work with LGBT prospective parents all over the world, I wonder what it will be like for their children to be the only ones or one of the few with queer parents in Wagoner, Okla., or Logansport, La., or Jerusalem, Israel. As adults we get to choose where we live and to what extent we want to be involved or identified with a queer community of some sort.

But is access to and participation in a community of LGBT parents and their kids an option or a necessity for our kids?

I hate to be elitist and say that all LGBT parents should raise their children in gay ghettos. But every teenage child of an LGBT parent to whom I have ever spoken talks painfully of their isolation and secrecy, or gratefully of the support and companionship of knowing other kids with gay parents. I also suspect that kids who grow up knowing other kids with LGBT parents are more comfortable with and accepting of LGBT people, including their parents. Increasing numbers of LGBT parents are moving their families to the suburbs. In many cases these families are having an extraordinarily positive impact on their mainstream communities, which may be meeting out gay people for the first time. Many rural and suburban LGBT parents believe their children experience little or no overt discrimination. (I find this somewhat hard to swallow, as homophobia is rife even in the schools of San Francisco and Cambridge.) I believe, however, that our kids deserve to have their queer heritage affirmed, not just politely overlooked as a nonissue.

It is crucial for all LGBT parents to make sure their kids know and have access to other kids with queer parents, and to ensure that their kids' teachers and principals recognize the importance of, and have the resources to, accurately include LGBT families and communities in all relevant contexts. It is one thing if our kids want to keep their parents' sexualities under wraps, but quite another thing for parents to directly or indirectly impose the closet on their kids or raise their children in a community where the closet is the only place they can feel safe.

We don't need to settle for trying to be like straight families. We can develop an LGBT family ethic and culture that transcends the weaknesses of the nuclear family and has a tremendous amount to offer society at large. Our reproductive circumstances force us to afford greater sensitivity to all family members' needs and a much wider range of options for defining family.

As I was growing up my enthusiasm about being Jewish ebbed and flowed, but I never thought being Jewish was something bad. When anti-Semitism crossed my path, I was able to recognize it for what it was rather than feeling exposed or ashamed. I knew there were some Jewish people and politics of which I was not proud. But I was always blessed with a critical sense of belonging to a substantial Jewish community and culture that I sought everywhere I lived and visited throughout the world. Being Jewish, a lesbian, and a feminist has been a combination of blessings and struggles that I would not have any other way. I feel confident about these aspects of my legacy to my daughter. When my daughter's dads and I decided to have her, we gave her not only life and three extended families, but also a rich, fun, creative, complex, politically conscious, and controversial LGBT heritage, community, and culture. We think these are among the greatest gifts we have to pass on to her.

Now that we know gay parenting is possible, LGBT parents and prospective parents must grow beyond the individual task of raising our own children—and on to embrace the collective responsibility of creating and being enriched by a greater community of LGBT families of which our children can be proud.

1. Some side effects of these drugs include hyperstimulation of the ovaries, hemorrhage, substantial weight gain, increased risk of cervical cancer, and others.

2. The cost of one in vitro fertilization procedure, which includes medication and sperm, runs between $8,500 and $10,000. The cost of gestational surrogacy, which includes expenses for the egg donor, carrier, legal arrangements, medications, and medical procedures, is approximately $40,000.

3. Gestational surrogacy involves a woman carrying a baby conceived from another woman's egg. Traditional surrogacy is when a woman carries a baby who was conceived from her own egg.

Spectrum of Parental Involvement

The following tool was designed to help Conception Connection clients identify their desired level of involvement with their biological child. Conversely, clients can identify clients of the opposite sex with whom they could conceivably construct a compatible arrangement. These categories are broad and are to be used only for initial identification of prospective parenting partners.

For the purpose of this exercise it might be helpful to define *parental rights and responsibilities* in terms of daily care, financial care, and decision making.

For Women	For Men
1. Surrogate mother who has no personal involvement.	1. Primary parent having a surrogacy agreement with a woman who has little to no personal involvement.
2. Biological mother who has involvement on level of a "family friend."	2. Primary parent where biological mother has involvement on the level of a "family friend."
3. Biological mother who has involvement on the level of an "aunt."	3. Primary parent where biological mother has involvement on the level of an "aunt."
4. Biological mother who has some limited parental rights and responsibilities.	4. Primary parent where the biological mother has limited parental rights and responsibilities.
5. Coparent equally sharing parental rights and responsibilities with the father(s).	5. Coparent equally sharing parental rights and responsibilities with the mother(s).
6. Primary parent where the biological father has limited parental rights and responsibilities.	6. Biological father with limited rights and responsibilities.
7. Primary parent where the biological father has involvement on the level of an "uncle."	7. Known sperm donor with involvement on the level of an "uncle."
8. Primary parent where the biological father has involvment on the level of a "family friend."	8. Known sperm donor with involvement on the level of a "family friend."
9. Primary parent having a donor agreement with a man who has little to no personal involvement.	9. Known sperm donor with little to no personal involvement.

Another Word for Matriarchy Is...
by Judy Grahn

Another word for matriarchy is *fantasy*.

For as long as lesbians have had a public movement with their own media, we have been fascinated by the idea of "matriarchy," consistently associated with stories of Amazon warriors and the recurrent myth of a golden age in which women "ruled." (For example, a 1974 grassroots publication, *Lesbians Speak Out*[1], included as part of a list of "books of interest to Lesbians" both Helen Diner's *Mothers and Amazons* and Elizabeth Gould Davis's *The First Sex*. These books explored the possibility that women once ruled societies.)

Yet no one has ever been able to find a matriarchy, past or present. Another word for matriarchy is *fantasy*, yet interest in it persists. Researchers in general describe societies that are matrilineal, meaning inheritance through the female line, and matrifocal, meaning daughters stay home, perhaps in the same living compound as their mothers.

People popularly use the term *matriarchy* to describe imagined lost queendoms ruled by women warriors, female social dominion, and also—on the Web—sexual games of dominance and submission, usually with a dominatrix and a man. In short, matriarchy is an archetype seeking to satisfy a widely felt hunger. Question is, hunger for what?

Perhaps *matriarchy* is a fantasy term based on desire for the female-active principle.

Historically, matriarchies never existed, for a simple reason: They did not need to. In matrilineal societies women had economic stability and political voice along with the men of their families, though the men may have had more public presence. In many systems, perhaps most, male power was vested in uncles and brothers, not husbands and fathers.

It is patriarchy that needed to be invented. Patriarchy is a particular historical form that needed to be invented and surrounded by rigorous laws and rules to hold it in place. In her book *The Creation of Patriarchy*, historian Gerda Lerner argues convincingly that the patriarchy that U.S. mainstream culture has inherited arose during the historic era of the second millennium B.C., or about 3,500 years ago, in Mesopotamia, among peoples who left us written records. Lerner demonstrates how the construction of patriarchy literally constructed forms of gender, dividing femaleness into two categories of sexuality—either "good" or "bad" women, along the lines of their sexual relation to "legitimate" paternity.

"Bad" women were sexually "unfaithful" to the principle of sacred paternity. This category has also included heterosexual "adulterous" women: "whores." Lesbianism has inherited this dualism. This may explain why lesbians are sometimes called "whores" as an expletive: The idea is that both categories of sexual behavior are unfaithful to the principle of patriarchal reproduction.

Patriarchy needed to be invented in order to sacralize and attempt to guarantee exact paternity and the functions of sperm in reproduction. While there are many varieties of patriarchy, and not all are oppressive, major patriarchal religions such as Christianity, Islam, and Judaism all share the refusal to sacralize the feminine. Recently women have demanded and persuaded some changes, such as use of the term *Mother-Father* to describe God and emphasis on Sophia as the Wisdom aspect of divinity. Despite these reforms the essential texts continue unrevised[2] and concentrate on stories of father-and-son relationships, the social responsibility and bonding of men, and the fidelity and goodness of women. The world into which patriarchy was borne took women's reproductive powers for granted; maternal powers were never in question. We always have known who the biological mother is. Though modern reproductive technology has changed even that, the biggest change, it seems to me, is that fatherhood need no longer be in question. Because of DNA testing, exact paternity can now be proven.

There is no longer reason for males to control the bodies of the women who father their children in order to establish lines of paternal inheritance. Social forms, however, will take time to catch up to technological advance. And it seems to me that as long as the sacred texts—Bible, Koran, and Torah—remain the primary source of sacred imagery, the patriarchal family will continue to try to dominate and assert itself to the exclusion of all other forms. I say "try" to dominate because when women have jobs, education, and money, conditions work in favor of their having choices and of families taking a variety of forms.

Another word for matriarchy is *hunger*: longing for something that is missing despite recent gains for women; something that has been missing for a long time. Perhaps the persistent hunger for matriarchy is hunger for divine images and writings about the female-active principle, for the sacralization of the feminine—not as "goodness and obedience," not as a dependent of the masculine, but as an active participant in culture, a leader in the directions of human life. To me, holding the feminine sacred honors all the bonds among women, including, but not exclusive of, the sexual bond between lover-partners.

That female powers of culture creation—the female-active principle—were firmly in place is evident from both the archeological findings of goddess icons and the widespread recognition of female deities in practices that continue in many cultures. She continues to be worshiped in some places despite continual encroachment of male-only religions. Unlike the monotheistic conception of a single male god, however, She was/is not alone. She took/takes an astounding variety of forms and had/has a lot of companion deities. This is what I love best about Her: She's a big variety girl, she can be a polydiversity principle.

If we define marriage as establishing the legitimacy of children—that is, establishing who is to take legal and economic responsibility—then when we look at family structures in place before the historic moment of the installation or evolution of patriarchy, with its particular imperatives, we see that families have organized themselves in a wide variety of forms. While popular anthropology may have tried to sell the idea that all peoples practice marriage identically in one-man/one-woman bonds, "marriage," like sexuality, is extremely diverse in its forms, as scientific anthropology acknowledges. Two male cousins and one wife (if she agrees) is a contemporary form for the Wodaabe people, nomadic pastoralists of Niger.[3]

Four sisters married to one husband was not unusual in Tibet or parts of India; five brothers marrying one woman is a typical bond in many portions of the globe. Among the Nuer people, for the purpose of establishing legal and economic responsibility for a child born to one woman, another woman would marry her—as a legal, not a sexual, bond. Also, the idea of who cannot marry has varied considerably and is open to change. Adoption and definitions of who is and is not part of "family" have also varied considerably, from severe restrictions to such openness as the Miwok people practiced on the West Coast: "Adoption could occur at any age as the result of instructions during a dream. A family would put beads around a person's neck, and he would be considered a relative."[4]

To a surprising extent societies and their economies have revolved around women's rituals just as much or more than men's rituals. Men's rituals—in India, for example—have thoroughly included the Sacred Feminine. Imagine the Super Bowl with players, coaches, and fans kneeling during halftime for a lengthy prayer to the Great Mother, who not only gave them life but is also the purpose, and perhaps the source of, their game.

"Widespread lesbianism in the U.S. is a result of the splintering of the extended family, an attempt among women to reconnect the fabric of society." I spoke this or a similar sentence while living in India recently, in response to a question about why we have so many lesbians in the U.S. I realized as I was speaking that I was not just trying to justify American behavior to a conservative people who value mother and father above all else. I was telling a truth about my own culture.

Lesbian and gay-male bonding, as I described in my book *Another Mother Tongue*, has had many uses in cultures at various times. I call these bondings lesbian and gay "offices," and they constitute an evolutionary capacity enhancing—even enabling—flexibility in human culture. Same-sex bonding can operate as a crossover agent, helping to move society from one set of rituals to another—from an outmoded, rigidified state into a fluid, forward-moving state. I call this evolutionary picture "braided evolution." Lesbian or gay "offices"—experienced at the personal level as "struggles"—can assist the accomplishment of a successful "braid." In this case the patriarchal family that began as a guarantee of exact fatherhood seems in many sectors to have run its course in this culture that values freedom and choice.

Another word for matriarchy is *Amazon*, and one meaning of Amazon may have been "motherlord."[5]

The underpinning of honoring "Earth Mother"—even in

conjunction with patriarchal religions—seems, from my research, to be related to acceptance of diversity, to solidarity of women, and to social justice. Lucia Birnbaum has found similar themes in her explorations of "black Madonnas" of Europe and North Africa. Archeologist Gimbutas thought that the societies that honored the sacred feminine of prehistoric Europe were matrilineal and that women held an edge of economic power,[6] a thesis confirmed by my own research in south India. Historian Lerner wrote: "No matter how degraded and commodified the reproductive and sexual power of women was (in ancient Mesopotamian life) their essential equality could not be banished from thought and feeling as long as the goddesses lived."[7] I personally believe that the re-establishment of a "motherlord" tradition of honoring the sacred feminine in nature, prehistory, and contemporary society is a prerequisite for expanding the participation of women in civil life and for changing definitions of family.

Placing the sacred feminine at the center of a relationship enables mutual respect for all the ways partners bond. This can move us beyond the sexual, psychological, and emotional to those longer-term homages that allow a relationship to stay in place for decades and decades. And that can allow a friendship to continue after a breakup.

If we think of the sacred feminine as a creation of women's collective consciousness and of our bonding with nature; if we place her at the center of our relationship, along with whatever formal religion we choose, we can know that she, as the magnetism of sexual love, created our bond. Created all the variety of bonds between women. Created our desire for each other. And she, especially as the collective feminine creator of culture, also created our differences. She makes us hungry for each other, helps bring us together, and perhaps can keep us together through life even should we split apart. For all the above reasons I advocate that women acquire education, jobs, and money; invest in community;

and honor the sacred feminine wherever possible.

1. This happens to be in my bookcase because I coedited it, but there are numerous other examples I could have used.

2. A major new story is in the poetry of Enheduanna, High Priestess of Ur in 2300 B.C.; complete translation is in Betty De Shong Meadoris Inanna's *Lady of Largest Heart*, University of Texas Press, fall 2000.

3. Beckwith, C. and Fisher, A. "African Marriage Rituals," *National Geographic*, Vol. 196, No. 5, November, 1999.

4. Heizer, R. (Ed.). *Handbook of North American Indians*, Vol. 8. Smithsonian Institution, 1978, p. 267.

5. From a Phoenician word. Sobol, D. *The Amazons of Greek Mythology*. London: A.S. Barnes, 1972.

6. Gimbutas, M. *The Civilization of the Goddess*. San Francisco: HarperSanFrancisco, 1991.

7. Lerner, p. 160.

Kate Kendell Wants Lesbians to Keep Their Promises
by Sarah Schulman

Kate Kendell is a very busy woman. She has a teenage daughter back in Utah and a girlfriend and a two-year-old son in San Francisco. She's also an attorney with a job that requires a lot of traveling and late hours. But most of her time these days is spent trying to understand the lesbian mind.

As executive director of the National Center for Lesbian Rights, Kate is at the forefront of recent court battles of a disturbing nature. It is not the religious right, not homophobic parents, and not disgruntled ex-husbands who are trying to deny basic parenting rights to lesbians. No, recently there have been more and more court cases involving lesbians who raised children in the context of a relationship, and once the relationship ended the biological mothers are going to court to keep their old girlfriends away from the children. On what grounds? These women are claiming that they never were a "family" as the courts understand that word, and that their ex-girlfriends are not eligible for the rights and responsibilities that a real family involves.

In this conversation I discuss with Kate the lesbian baby boom, with its origins and psychological underpinnings; the specific issues of interracial couples in relationship to parenting; and, finally, why lesbians would undermine 30 years of gay family law just to hurt their ex-lovers, and what the rest of us can do about it.

Why Lesbians Are Having Children

S: Why do so many gay women want to have children?

K: I think there are a number of factors. My experience, personally, has to do with a social imperative more for women than there is for men—for women to be mothers, to be nurturers. Because there is that social imperative, or maybe the social imperative springs up because there is a natural sense. I don't know which comes first.

S: But why now, if it's "natural," and not ten years ago?

K: Because ten years ago virtually every lesbian bought into—illegitimately, based on heavy social pressure—the construct that you couldn't be a lesbian and a parent. The only way it could happen was if you had kids in a heterosexual marriage. The vast majority of gay kids being raised by lesbian [or] gay parents right now were the product of a heterosexual marriage.

S: Are you saying that the separation between sexuality and gender role was artificial?

K: I think there is an artificiality and a compulsion to both. What I feel we've achieved is we've mostly eradicated the disfavor of lesbians having children in the lesbian community—it's sort of [the mind-set of] "Whatever you want to do." We've come to a neutral place. I think that's a good thing. It's a personal choice, and we shouldn't care based on a politic. Now we can't still do anything about the fact that there is a compulsion in the society at large that women have to have children and be nurturers. I think that should be neutral too. But obviously that's not going to happen. So now the artificiality doesn't come from a lesbian community saying having kids buys into patriarchy. It really all comes from a society that says women should have babies and be nurturers. And I think there are a lot of lesbians who are having kids, almost always because they sincerely want to, but who are hearing that message loud and clear, and there is no actual counterbalance to that message.

S: Is the lesbian baby boom partially the product of a more conservative set of gender roles?

K: That's right.

S: There's no discussion or critique of that.

K: There's not, and in fact, if you do discuss it or critique it as Kate Clinton has done, people are uncomfortable. I am a parent myself. I was a parent essentially by accident. I fell in love with a woman who had a one-year-old daughter. Emily was almost a year old when her mother and I got involved. And we were together 11 years, and I, over that time, became a parent to Emily as well. So now I have a kid graduating from high school. And then Sandy and I have a 2½-year-old son. On both scores my role as a parent, while intentional, has been not something I've yearned for with a hope and a desperation and a yearning that some other women bring to it.

S: Given all the instability in lesbian relationships and all the custody problems you've been facing, and that most people are going to end up being single mothers ultimately or reconfiguring their family, isn't there some way this parenting within a couple may be a model that is somewhat more imitative than what may end up as the reality of what a lesbian family is going to look like?

K: I think that couples who are no longer together, the majority are navigating raising the child quite successfully. Maybe it's still based on a heterosexual model—that is, a couple gets divorced and they share custody or they share visitation—but it's the model that has been institutionalized in our society because there is quite a bit of documentary evidence that it's in the child's best interest to approximate the same relationship the child had with both parents as if they were [still] living under one roof. To navigate that for a child and keep the other person involved in the child's life—share custody or visitation…to make sure that's all healthy, an additional piece of the matrix would be that the two adult people would go on to have healthy adult relationships. That's normal. That happens all the time.

Biracial Parenting

S: The other day I was at this birthday party, and the scene was interracial lesbian couples with kids. Of the four or five couples there, most of the women had decided to have biracial kids. If the black woman was the mother, she had a white or light-skinned donor, and if the white woman was the mother, she had a donor of color, it being difficult to get black donors who will give permission to be contacted later by the child. I was really interested in this because, in a way, it's an imitation of sexual reproduction. No one is going to think that one impregnated the other. The child is never going to think that they are a genetic mix. So it seems like one of many complex aspects of a kind of a transitional phase—people still trying to figure out the father role.

K: That's an interesting observation, and it's one that mirrors my own family. I think that the best explanation I can give for it is that to some degree it may be imitative; that doesn't make it wrong or improper, because having children in a context of a couple is imitative itself. Having a family that lives together under one roof is imitative. I don't know if it's transitional to something else or if it's just a desire to approximate as closely as possible what society understands and recognizes, and thereby hope for some additional measure of acceptance or ease for our families.... Sandy and I chose to have a biracial child, recognizing that to some degree that would be more difficult, although in [San Francisco] it is much less unusual; biracial children are very much the norm in all sorts of families here. Part of the reason [we had a biracial child] is that we didn't see ourselves as a statistic that would not be together. And we, particularly Sandy, wanted to have a child [situation in which] both of us, in terms of our genetic backgrounds and our ethnicity, were part of him, if not actually part of the gene pool. Because we see ourselves, of course, in the bliss of love, being together and raising him to adulthood. That is our family, that's who each of us is, and he is the product of each of us coming together. I'm sure, with a few hours of real intensive therapy, we may uncover some more stuff, but that's all I can give you at this point. [*Laughs.*]

The Father Role

S: I think it has to do more with the father role, which no one can figure out. The straight father role. Most people have been disappointed by their fathers. Fathers have not worked out.

K: No—in general, for almost everybody.

S: Now the "other mother," who is the person that you're very concerned with in your legal work, is in this very peculiar position of trying to fill a role that is actually false in the first place. In many cases it may just be revealing that the birth mother or whatever you call it—"the bio mother–child bond"—is *the* bond. The other person may on some level just be the visitor, which is the way many of us felt about our own fathers.

K: What lesbian couples do is parenting, regardless of the psychology of how they're filling the "father" role and how they're figuring [who] the donor's going to be, whatever that piece of the puzzle is. My sense is that that [father] role serves one purpose, and that is to create a child—if you're having a child, through pregnancy, I [as a woman] can't provide that. Once that's done, I get to be a parent in whatever way I want. I get to create as much involvement and as much caring place for me in my son's life as I want. It is completely up to me to script it. And I don't have to, nor would I ever, buy into a role that is really anything that's on the margins.

S: Most of us have had weird fathers, and yet, there is this exaltation of the father role. And now the other mother is in this very undefined place, and this biracial couple/biracial child idea is, in a way, a simulacra role. It's like pretending that it's your sperm, or pretending that you are identified by whiteness—[pretending] that that is the marker of who you are. It feels like something that people will look back on later as an idea just getting started, in its first phases.

K: Most of my friends in interracial couples who have chosen to have a biracial child…have chosen this because they want the rest of the world to be able to look at either one of them and say that either one could be the parent, so that neither one feels isolated or marginalized based on appearance.

So that the African-American parent or the Latina parent can take the child to the grocery store and people won't think, particularly because she's African-American or Latina, that she's the nanny.

S: And in your case people would think, *Oh, she had sex with a black man*, but actually you had sex with a black woman, and that had nothing to do with the birth of the child. So the whole racist fantasy of that is recreated and projected. Although having sex with a black woman does not carry the same social meaning for a white woman as it does to have sex with a black man.

K: Not in larger society nor in lesbian culture. When people are having this discussion, it is interesting how white privilege gets involved in it. I've known white parents who had no compulsion whatsoever taking their child, who may be fully African-American, to the grocery store, where no one would assume she was the nanny. And yet it becomes maybe a more important issue for the woman of color in the relationship because of the larger racism in the society.

S: There is more design in lesbian reproduction than for straights.

K: I suppose the end point of the discussion is that lesbian couples who choose to have children—either through adoption [or,] particularly, through pregnancy—as a biracial couple make choices about what the child's going to look like and who the child's going to be, [which] can be based on all sorts of superficial factors and appearance factors that may or may not play out in the way they thought they were going to. What it shows is how incredibly influential the larger society is.

Custody

S: The same women, the lesbian biological mothers, now who are using the state to keep children from their ex-girl-friends previously would have had their kids taken away if they had been with men. Now they are "the man" because they have the state on their side. It's about who's got the phal-lus. Is it just that people are so corruptible that as soon as you have the power of the state you start bullying others? And that the earlier experience of being marginalized has no impact?

K: That's a very cynical but I think—sadly—pretty accurate assessment. Any other explanation is even more cynical. If it's not that these biological parents simply are using power just because they've got it, then it has to do with something about the lesbian bio parent psyche, which could be about owner-ship—a sense of a child as property.

S: Does it have to do with their sense of their own feminin-ity, or being "a real woman," because they have a child?

K: Clearly we all have this sense, and probably all have an experience growing up where we got the message that if you are a mother and you got divorced, you should have custody, you should seek custody, you should want it, and if you didn't, there's something wrong with you. But what these bio parents are doing is so beyond that, because in most of these cases no one is saying that the biological parent doesn't get custody. She will. She does. It is generally conceded by the other par-ent. All the non–bio parent wants is to fill the shoes of what is a very common and easily recognizable model, the true non-custodial-father model. She's the noncustodial parent. She'll have visitation every other weekend and on Wednesday evenings—that's the standard rule—and will have some role in the child's life. This is a model that we've seen billions of times in every heterosexual divorce in which children were involved. It's not as if we're saying to biological mothers, "You need to accept an entirely different model because you're a lesbian family" or that she needs to give up something more than a heterosexual woman would have to give up. No, what we're saying is that we should play by the same rules. These biological mothers are saying, "No, we don't have to play by the same rules because the legal system doesn't recognize what I have as a family. So I'm not going to recognize it as a family, either, because it is no longer convenient for me to do so."

S: What is the psychology of that?

K: For the women who do this, it is classic victim psychology that puts them in a position of fighting for the illegitimate because of past victimization or internalized homophobia or a sense of themselves as really out of the protection of the larger society. It's a sense of completely not getting it and not understanding the ultimate harm.

S: That's ideological, but what about emotionally? The only times in their lives they've ever had any state power is because they became mothers. All their lives they were treated as lesbians—suddenly they're being treated as straight women. But the person on the other side is not a man.

K: No, she's a lesbian and she is really not the outsider. It is a sense of being able to victimize the victim.

S: Have you interviewed any of these people that you opposed in court?

K: I've talked to several of them. What they say is, "Well, she never really was a parent. She never wanted to be a parent. I never considered her to be a parent." It's all postjustifications for why she's taking the position she's taking.

S: Do they believe that, or do they know they are lying about the past?

K: Whether they wake up at 3 o'clock in the morning and feel sick to their stomach because they know they are perpetuating a huge charade, I don't know.

S: How many cases are there right now of lesbians denying their lovers access to the child they both raised?

K: Around the country we know of a dozen cases. As soon as some get resolved for better or for worse, there are cases to replace it.

Why Lesbians Can Behave So Badly, and How Their Friends Can Change It

S: Why do some lesbians do things to their lovers that are so sinister and twisted that it reaches a degree no one else seems to be able to equal?

K: I used to say that these cases broke my heart, because I expected and wanted so much more from women in my community. If someone would have said to me before I knew about this phenomenon that this was happening and it is probably going to happen a lot more, I would not have believed them.

S: Look, you're talking about lesbians—people who are asocialized, who are in many ways outside the norms of the society, so perhaps people act in a way as if they don't care about the consequence, they don't care about how they are viewed—because they don't feel any stake in social agreement or social order, even within a lesbian community. If you feel no one is watching, that no one is protecting you, that no one has an expectation of you, then you can act in this very destructive manner.

K: And you can convince yourself that taking a parent away from your child doesn't do damage to that child? That is the thing that I'm most baffled by. How can you say that a seven-year-old, who calls this person "Mama" and has seen her every single day of her life, should be told one day that she's never going to see Mama again? I don't care what this woman's socialization is.

S: I know you don't like the behavior; I agree it's disgusting. But let's think about why this is happening. Why are so many lesbians willing to act so crazily and destructively when not a single gay man has gone to court to deny his ex-lover visitation of their child?

K: It comes from a place that is so victimized that you don't even understand when you've moved from being the victim to the oppressor, and being able to justify it. I'm convinced that the reason most of these cases proceed is that, by and large, most women who take this position do have a cadre of friends supporting them. Most of them are not completely alone. They usually have a cadre of close friends who say, "Oh, yeah, she was a bitch. I never liked her," not appreciating that there is a child in the center of this family. Generally, the biological parents who take this position have at least a handful of other lesbians who support her in her actions. The community needs to be able to put sufficient pressure on the bio mom's friends to tell her, "We can't support you in this strategy."

S: That's what makes you so interesting, Kate—your community-based approach to this, since the relationship between lesbians and the court system [or] lesbians and the state is an ever-changing and totally undependable relationship. A caring, responsible, ethical, involved community becomes the only response to people's destructive behavior—to make amoral lesbians realize that, actually, someone does care about how they act and that there is someone who notices and cares enough that the woman in question has to be accountable; to tell her that she does live within a moral system.

K: I'll use whatever I have to. I think these cases are so ultimately destructive, and, given the failure of the legal system to catch up, I and other advocates will use whatever we have to try to protect our families, our family law, and these kids. We must stop bio moms from taking this position.

S: OK, but let's separate out the issue of children for a moment and look at the larger moral question and the strategy you're using. You're taking a group of people, lesbians, [whom] nobody cares about…. When something bad happens to them there is no one to protect them, and when they are doing something wrong there is no one to intervene and tell them that they shouldn't—people who have lived in an emotionally anarchistic state. So basically I can do anything nasty to you, and no one is going to tell me it's not OK and no one is going to help you. We have relationships that are illusions of safety, but we don't have family support and we don't have societal support. We're floating emotional satellites. What you're trying to do is to anchor this behavior by creating a community responsibility so that if someone is acting immorally, their friends will intervene. Do you think that that can be used on other terms besides children?

K: It can be used for good or for ill. It is a strategy that is very risky.

S: Why?

K: Because [if] you live in Utah [as I do] and you're a member of ACT UP and you chain yourself to Temple Square trying to give light to the antigay activities of the [Mormon] Church, [but] your friends are saying, "Stop it, you're causing too much trouble and making it hard for us," that is an unfortunate use of community pressure.

S: On the other hand, if your family was abusively homophobic, would it, based on your concept of the community, be my responsibility to go to your family of origin and tell them their behavior is not acceptable because I am in a community that is accountable to you? If I'm going to condemn you when you're horrible, I also have to defend you when someone else is treating you unfairly, right?

K: It gives some substance to the word *community* to think that there would be such an ethic and sense of responsibility. Whenever I talk about the queer "community" I think of the quotation marks in my head. I don't know that there really is a queer community—the word connotes a collective responsibility, collective caretaking, collective concern for the welfare of those who are members. I think we've got a community in only the loosest sense. But virtually every member of the queer community has their own little community of friends that can have influence.

Being Responsible and Accountable to Each Other

S: Have you ever gone to the birth families of any of your friends and told them their homophobia toward your friend was inappropriate?

K: Nope.

S: Would you be willing to?

K: Yes. Part of what the issue is for taking on a sense of community responsibility is that you have to have nothing to lose yourself. Even our suggesting that there should be community pressure on these biological moms to not take this position—well, the only way that's going to happen is if people have nothing to lose or see it in their self-interest.

S: But they will have something to lose. And as my friend Allison Gross reminds me, standing up for somebody else is uncomfortable. People will allow almost any evil to occur rather than be uncomfortable.

K: True, we don't behave that way.

S: But we could.

K: We could. We at NCLR think that [in] this particular situation…setting up a sense that there should be a community standard opposed to bio moms doing this is in the best interests of the broader community.

S: Because there are children involved. But what if there were just adults involved? What if it was in the best interests of lesbians?

K: They still should treat each other honorably and abide by their promises to each other.

S: But if you've been told your whole life that you are worthless, what good is your word? When we did the Lesbian Avengers, one of the things I learned there was that we had a constituency of people, many of whom had been told all their lives that they were nothing. Many had never had or used power, did not know how to be proactive, felt their only power was to be obstructive. A lot of times, lesbians would come into a room determined that the only way they could express themselves was to stop something. We had to create a rule that if you disagreed with a proposal, you couldn't just critique it, you had to make a better suggestion. This drove people wild because they didn't have the skill or authority to be proactive and create things, to negotiate, to face and deal with problems, to propose solutions. Some already had these skills, many learned how to be constructive, and some are, this day, unable to have agency.

Let's take your idea and expand it. What you are talking about is a real gay family. If you are in a functional straight family and your husband is treating you like shit, your brother might drive over to the house and tell him that that's not OK. But if it's your girlfriend, nobody gives a shit. Your family is not going to do anything, and your "friends" are going to stay out of it. You're alone. If we want to have a gay family that is equal to the straight family, we need to have an ethic of intervention and accountability that functions along the lines of their official ethic at its most functional. What you are doing is the beginning of something that can really transform what our lives are like.

K: [If] you've got somebody who's not going to allow visitation; you go over there, you sit down, and you tell them, "This isn't OK." The reason that tactic can work, and the reason I suggest it, is because I've seen women insulated by their friends. I know if they lose the last bit of cover they've got— those few close friends who are all they've got left—supporting them in an immoral action, it is a very rare person who will say "Fuck you all, I'll fly by myself." It is a rare person who won't succumb to some degree to close friends saying, "You can't do this," wanting her to be a moral person.

S: Because our friends are all we have.

K: Yes.

S: So, basically, if someday…a woman tries to keep her kid away from his or her other parent, the community can intervene; if someone's family is abusively homophobic to them, the community can intervene; if your lover is abusive and destroying the fabric of your life, the community can intervene. In other words, we can have a social structure.

K: That's exactly right. We don't have a social structure. The legal system does not simply require that we play by the same rules as heterosexual couples. Eventually the system will do that, but until they catch up I can't demand that bio moms always be rational, because they're not going to be. The only thing we've got left is to say that friends will intervene and say, "You can't do this. We're not going to support this." It is in the long-term best interest of the child, the couple, and the community. If the community could really take responsibility about us being honorable to each other, then it doesn't matter what the legal system does, then we don't have to pay tens of thousands of dollars to attorneys. There's actually more certainty, and it's less wrenching if there is a sense of responsibility. We are responsible for the decisions we make with each other.

S: People have been willing to advocate for each other politically. People who don't have AIDS fight for people who do. People who haven't been fired work for nondiscrimination.

But now it has to go into the emotional arena. People will throw blood on the White House and go to jail, but they won't go to their friend's house and say, "The way you're treating your girlfriend is completely unacceptable." Why is that?

K: It must be a sense that we consider that "private."

S:"Private" means the heterosexual family. "Private" means that Mommy, Daddy, the three children, and Aunt Louise are going to discuss this. In lesbian life there is nobody else there. "Private" means you're alone in your house with no one to stand up for you or to intervene. There is no such thing as "private"—it means isolation.

K: We import the construct from a heterosexual model.

S: Where it meant Daddy's prerogative.

K: We do not have systems that force us to be accountable, even if we hate each other. We have the potential to do enormous psychological damage that heterosexuals can never do, because the law doesn't let them.

The Latest Lesbian Villain
by Nom de Plum

Am I prepared to identify myself, even in an article written under an alias, as the latest lesbian villain, the biological mother who "pulls rank"? As more lesbian biological mothers are opting to refuse visitation to their former partners, "biological mom bashing" has become commonplace. We are morally bankrupt kidnappers, drunk with power, hell-bent on destroying family ties to serve our own twisted needs for power and control. With the accusatory, self-righteous finger of the lesbian community pointed firmly in my direction, is it any wonder that I balk at presenting a viewpoint that many will consider high treason? Yet these are exactly the methods that our rigid and judgmental community has employed to silence unpopular, politically incorrect views for decades.

We are at a crossroads. After breaking up with their partners, a significant number of lesbian biological mothers are refusing joint custody and/or visitation arrangements and deciding to parent alone. The community can either continue its scapegoating or begin the journey toward understanding. I will write. Walk with me for a while in my shoes.

We met, moved in, and married in less than one year. Not until after I became pregnant did I discover that my partner suffered from a serious mental illness. Every day I rode the roller coaster of her explosive anger, grandiosity, depression, and mania. When Catherine[1] arrived, the situation worsened. An infant has no defense against an adult's rage. The notion that we were going to jointly and equally coparent evaporated. My former partner was too caught up in her own needs to care for a child and resented my doing so. I was parenting both of them.

Catherine and my former partner did not bond. I can still remember my daughter crawling away from her as fast as her young knees could carry her. As she grew, I found it increasingly difficult to protect her from my partner's instability. By the time my daughter was one year old, I knew I had to separate.

Divorce can be a devastating experience, and lesbian divorce even more so. After I moved out Catherine contracted a serious illness. Then my car broke down, and I had to rely on friends to transport her to the doctor's office. I missed day after day of work, jeopardizing my new job. My former partner did not help us through this difficult time. Instead she waited to assert her "parental rights" until we were in the midst of negotiating the division of our joint property. These rights, of course, did not include any responsibilities such as providing child support or caring for Catherine when she was sick.

I faced an ethical dilemma. As the sole support for our household I was required to work and commute a combined ten hours a day during the week. Catherine hated these separations. Now I was being asked to give up my weekends, my only free time with Catherine, to provide visitation to my former partner. Visitation, even supervised, raised serious safety concerns. Since the breakup, my former partner's behavior had become increasingly obsessive and bizarre.

On the other hand, I knew that if we had been a heterosexual couple, I would not have been able to make this choice unilaterally. Instead, it would have been the subject of a custody battle. Given my former partner's mental instability, the outcome might have been the same, but the process would have financially and emotionally bankrupted me.

I looked at my daughter. Since the breakup she had never even mentioned my former partner's name. Was this visitation really for her? Theory said yes, but reality said otherwise. So I did the unthinkable. I said no.

To do what was best for Catherine, I took advantage of how the law treats our families differently. I recognize this may seem morally repugnant to those who believe we should be struggling to obtain for lesbians the same legal treatment to which heterosexual couples comply. I acknowledge that many situations exist in which refusing to permit visitation between a child and the child's nonbiological mother is completely unjustified and grossly unfair. This issue, however, is far too complex to be resolved by a position that paints all lesbian families with the same broad brush or adopts the current state of the law governing heterosexual families as the ideal. It is an easy out to explain the ever-growing number of lesbian biological mothers refusing visitation to their former partners as "bad girls." As in most situations, the truth lies not in the black-and-white, but somewhere in the gray.

While my lesbian coparenting experience was unusual due to my former partner's mental illness, I would like to comment on some of the subtler dynamics of my experience that I suspect are far more common. First, I do not believe it is any coincidence that my experience as a lesbian biological mother and partner had a lot in common with the stereotypical experience of being a traditional heterosexual mother and wife. Gender roles are a societal fact, and this fact still holds true in same-sex relationships. Indeed, in recent years the lesbian community has witnessed a revival of butch/femme role-playing with its attendant gender-based stereotyping.

While I am aware that truly egalitarian coparenting relationships exist, as the biological mother in a lesbian couple I found myself typecast in the traditional mother/wife role, while my partner played the role of the father/husband. I was expected to take on the lion's share of child raising with little appreciation or assistance. My former partner could, and often did, choose to exit when the going got tough, then return for the smooth sailing. Interestingly, I often heard this complaint among the lesbian biological mothers within my circle of friends. When this sort of dynamic leads to minimal bonding with the child and a feeling that the biological mother is already parenting alone, it is easy to see why lesbian biological mothers would choose to sever ties with the nonbiological parent after a breakup. While traditional heterosexual men have been doing this for years and are still accorded full rights and privileges in the event of divorce, I suspect that lesbians have higher expectations of equality and are less tolerant of being exploited in this manner.

During our breakup I once again found myself in the traditional female role. I was confronted with a "deadbeat dad" who was exerting her parental rights to extort financial concessions from me in our property negotiations. She appeared to regard Catherine as a piece of property to which she had acquired ownership interest. She made demands but offered nothing in return. While my former partner had the ability to finance prolonged legal negotiations, I was struggling to hang on to my job and cover the extraordinary costs of Catherine's day care and medical expenses.

I understand that if this had been a heterosexual divorce, no father would have lost his visitation privileges for behaving in such a manner. The solution, however, does not lie in advocating across-the-board oppression. The equality ideal demands more. Until that occurs I predict that lesbian biological mothers in this situation will continue to "pull rank" with or without community approval.

1. Characteristics that would reveal the identity of the family described in this article have been changed to protect their privacy.

The Changes Wrought:
How Parenting Is Changing Lesbian Culture
by Jess Wells

Queer parents and the press surrounding our increasing numbers frequently mention how we're changing the shape of the American family, but what is just as startling is how lesbian parenting is changing the shape of lesbian culture. From our romances and our relationships with our families to our sense of connection to the world, our children are radically changing our community.

Changing Our Love

Consider first the way the baby boom is impacting our romantic relationships. Suddenly in lesbian dating, one's suitability as a parent is a factor in choosing a lover. Straight women for millennia have considered one type of lover acceptable for fun but have looked elsewhere for a "good father" for their children. They have built into their culture a potential compromise between love and parenting. At the very least, it's been on their list of requirements. Lesbians have never been faced with those considerations before. Lesbians have never had to navigate the mysterious ground between lust, love, intimacy, commitment, parenting, and permanence. And, frankly, I think, over the next 20 years the result will be that we're not going to be very good at it. We'll be in relationships in which we'll assume that someone will be a good parent just because she is the love of our life...then we'll discover otherwise.

This should make us very circumspect in the call for the recognition of a permanent bond between parents—a lifelong, legally binding relationship—and I think we have to recognize that it would be the first adult relationship in the entire history of lesbian culture that could not be voluntarily dissolved. Our "marriages" are voluntary, our chosen families are voluntary, our definitions of ourselves as queer, even our gender is voluntary, mutable, temporary. If queer marriage were legal, queer divorce would be as well. The fluidity in which we live has its downside, surely—lack of rights, the homophobia that drives the refusal to allow us marry, some wickedly nasty custody battles—but we also must acknowledge that this fluidity has given our culture a tremendous ability to invent better systems, to create better ways to live. As we look at families that break up amid strife over custody, it's important to remember that this is the first time in our history that parenting has played into our love relationships and the first time that we as a culture have been faced with a call for utter and absolute permanence. We are going to be clumsy with it for quite a while.

For example, I have met women who have given birth to children outside of their current relationship, then gone through second-parent adoptions as a way to pledge their love to their new partner, using custody as a substitute for legal marriage. I have met women who have needed reassurance that dating someone doesn't automatically make them a parent to the children, that it's OK to have a lover who is not suddenly enmeshed in every facet of their life. Boundaries have never been our culture's strongest suit, and parenting is making it even more confusing.

As a result, the baby boom and its sudden insertion into our romances is going to slow down the infamous moving-van syndrome in which lesbians box up their lives and move in on the second date. It may not take longer than two dates to determine whether you're sexually, politically, and socially compatible. But it takes a lot longer than that to hash out the fine points of parenting, especially since we currently have no dialogue or process to discuss it. The lesbian parenting movement will make us more circumspect and slow us in our mad dash toward domestication. And after our kids are born we'll slow down in our hunt for girlfriends because our kids need us to go slowly—you just can't put your kid's heart on the line too often. We'll have to date without introducing the girlfriend to our kids, to make sure the relationship is going to go somewhere, then slowly introduce the two sides of our lives and deal with the jealousy and the fallout. Many single mothers I know swear that they'll never live with a lover until the kids are gone because they can't subject their children to the uncertainty. Besides, kids require a lot of time, and baby-sitters cost a lot of money, so the whole process of dating a mother takes much longer.

Parenting is also challenging what I consider a cultural obsession with equality and sameness. Lesbians tend to assume that sameness is the key to equality and that equality is essential for nonoppressive relationships. But parents are discovering otherwise. Someone is breast-feeding and someone else feels left out, and what we're discovering is that's OK, because breast milk for the baby is more important than the parents feeling equal. You discover other inequalities when you date a woman with a child: Suddenly she has to call a lot of the shots, and that's OK—because the kid not watching violent TV (or getting home in time for bed, or determining which night you go to a show based on the sitter's schedule) is more important than a single woman's freedom to do whatever she wants whenever she wants it.

In fact, I think one of the contributions that will grow out of the lesbian community in the next 20 years is the idea that perhaps romantic love is not the best foundation for a family. Let's face the facts: Our relationships break up. We remain tremendous friends, members of the chosen family. And as lesbians with limited resources (and because we're damn smart) we build support systems of multiple godparents, aunts, and uncles. We build an extended family. It would be helpful, both to lesbian love and to lesbian families, to not try so hard to replicate the two-parent patriarchal model and keep everyone else at bay. What would it do to our relationships, our romance, our families if we made families with people who were good parenting material regardless of whether they slept in our bed? As we became more comfortable with change we could allow romantic love to dissolve when it needs to and find places in the extended family for everyone who loves the child, regardless of title. In the extended family there's room for both permanence and fluidity.

A case could be made that parenting is actually changing the *type* of love that is exchanged within some lesbian relationships. Cut off from the opportunity to nurture at the level that children need nurturing, some lesbians have turned their attention to adults, who should not actually require nurturing at that level or to that extent. Hence, the overly involved, joined-at-the-hip, adult-child-of-an-alcoholic, rescuing type of relationship. I've met lesbians who report that their relationships with adults are healthier now that they have children because they have someone who really needs them to be tremendously involved, who actually needs their constant attention. As a result, they suddenly insist that adults stand on their own two feet. And it's not too far a leap to wonder what might happen to our obsession with our cats and our dogs if we were finally and truly free to parent.

But the most startling impact on lesbian love has been the introduction of the overwhelming, indescribable love a parent feels for her child. Lesbian parents find themselves infused with love on the cellular level. Our culture has been cut off from what is the most profound love on the planet: the love of a parent for a child. When I see how deep, total, and passionate the love is, how transformative it is, I am furious with homophobes who have cut us off from this love for so long.

As a corollary, the risk your heart takes in parenting is enough to bring you to your knees. When you're the mother of a one or a two-year-old who is suddenly making strides into the world, you realize that if your child died, you really wouldn't want to live. You pray that if your child has to die, then the two of you will die together in each other's arms. And you know that if you had the misfortune of outliving your child, you'd go absolutely crazy with grief. I've loved women very deeply in my life, but I've never had my sanity and my fundamental desire to live tied to another human being as it is with my child.

Changing Our Relationships to Our Families

Much has been said, and most of it negative, about our change in status within our families of origin when we have kids. Suddenly grandparents are on planes visiting us, treating us like someone who has done something normal for once. It does help with communication, I have found. My own mother and I got along much better after the birth of my son because we suddenly had something neutral to talk about. Like men who talk about sports with their fathers, my mother and I found a common ground in becoming my son's fan club. But I have found that improvement in status is short-lived. Once the baby is a toddler, there appears to be second-generation homophobia, in which grandparents worry about his hair being too long, why he might be wearing beads or nail polish to school, why they can't buy him toy guns. Suddenly the grandparents are visiting your sister's kids more than yours, and the pain of exclusion is even greater than the way they used to slight you, because they're hurting the little one you can't bear to see hurt.

But that is *their* reaction to *us*. What surprised me as a result of becoming a parent was my reaction to them. I discovered that parenting is far too risky an endeavor if it doesn't include a sense of forgiveness. If we can't forgive our parents for their mistakes, then there's no forgiveness in the world at all, and by extension we will not be forgiven for the mistakes we're making with our children. I'm not saying we can forgive our parents for child abuse; I can't really forgive my mother for dying of alcoholism. But there's a day-to-day forgiveness that is a gift. As mothers doing the best we can and knowing that sometimes it's not the best that can be done, we have to have a sense of forgiveness. And that forgiveness is a great relief, really. I realized after the birth of my son that the question was no longer how good or bad a mother my own mother had been. The only question was how good a mother I was going to be. It put an end to a lifelong struggle. It took a tremendous weight off my shoulders, and it occurs to me now that by cutting us off from parenting the patriarchy has denied us the natural segue that straight people have used. It has cordoned us off and trapped us in the seemingly endless spiral of resentment, blame, and longing.

With this comes a newfound sense of gratitude. When we see firsthand the amount of work and self-sacrifice that is required to parent, we are blessed with thankfulness. After yet another dinner of hot dogs, another Saturday night spent in front of *The Jungle Book*, another newspaper not read, another day in the same old jeans because you need money for his books, you remember that at one point somebody did this for you.

It's remarkable how parenting gives you back your childhood. Better yet, it gives you the opportunity to keep what was good about your childhood and eliminate the bad. It makes you remember things you liked to do that you hadn't thought of in years, and gives you permission to do them. My personal favorites are swinging upside down, root beer barrel candy, Sponge Bob SquarePants cartoons, and stomping on sand castles immediately upon completion. Parenting teaches you how to play, to take delight in the truly simple pleasures.

Changing Our Connections to Our Bodies

In this era gay people regard our bodies almost as we do the atomic bomb: a catastrophic force outside our control, able to destroy us without warning. Bodily fluids are the enemy. Into this scenario come the lesbian mothers, whose breast milk is not only a nontoxic substance but something essential for immune systems, digestion, and, now they're discovering, for intellectual development as well. In this era of AIDS it was a surprise to stock my fridge with frozen bodily fluids for someone else's survival.

The process of pregnancy puts us in touch with a set of forces within our bodies that we didn't know about before. During the first trimester of pregnancy our relationship to food changes. Hunger isn't something that makes us feel proud that we're burning calories. Hunger becomes a panicked feeling, caused by a fetus that knows that every minute it doesn't have nourishment is a minute that it's starting to die. In the last trimester our hip joints soften and our pubic bones spread and we fall into a nonlinear stupor that midwives say is nature's way of teaching us to shift our focus from the practical world to nonverbal communication with the baby. There is no more primal experience (that you survive, anyway) than giving birth, and when you do you are transformed into the cave-dwelling mother bear: a protective isolationist afraid to leave the den. I was emotionally unable to have my baby out of my arms for more than 20 minutes when he was born: Nature's clock was making sure he was nursed at regular intervals. You are suddenly an animal.

Changing Our Relationship to Culture

Critics of the lesbian parenting community maintain that we are given additional privileges in society as a result of having children, and while I've certainly felt that strangers are more friendly and accepting of me when they stop to admire my child, I've also been struck by the opposite phenomenon: the increase in vulnerability. The right wing is at war with lesbian parents. We are their final battle. Fear is more a condition of our parenting than nearly any other social group: fear of having our children taken away, fear of being attacked on the street, fear of our children being scapegoated at school. Situations that are mildly troublesome or somewhat precarious for a nonparent become outright dangerous for us: Running out of gas on the freeway, we cannot walk the shoulder clutching a four-year old. Harassed on the street for a "Dykes Rule" button on our lapel, we cannot flee carrying a 50-pound five-year-old or roll up our sleeves and fight. Busted for a roach in the ashtray, a lesbian mother is in danger of losing her children. If we seem more closeted, it's because we are more endangered, more vulnerable, with much, much more to lose.

But on the positive side, I have found one of the greatest gifts of parenthood is its sense of accountability. There's this little spirit watching you, expecting the best from you. You were going to get your habits under control—someday—but suddenly that day is here. I am more patient, more generous, less angry, and more clean and sober than I ever thought I would be—because I want to show him the way. I want to model the best behavior I possibly can, for him—and he will never know how much I thank him for demanding the best of me. So what can we expect of a community that is suddenly held accountable and that rises to the challenge?

After becoming a mother I had an almost physical sense of connection to the past and the future. I thought I had been a concerned environmentalist and a good political lesbian, but I wasn't prepared for the new intensity and depth of my commitment to the future as a place where my son and my son's children would live. I also was not prepared to suddenly feel part of a lineage: the past and the future flowing through me like a cord, tying me to a sense of belonging.

That belonging deepens our commitment to our own lives and safety because we are startled into realizing that we cannot die and orphan our children. We drive more carefully, because being seriously injured would impact not just us, but our kids. Suicide, dying young, giving up is no longer that lurking option in the deep corner that you didn't even know was an option until parenting makes you realize that it is completely out of the question.

In terms of a cultural impact, though, I think we should stop to ask ourselves what it will mean to our community to bring truly queer kids into the world. Regardless of their affectional preference, we are raising kids within the queer community. In the past our culture has been built of people who are produced and raised by heterosexuals who then migrated to queer culture. What does it mean to our cultural makeup to now contribute to our own gene pool, our own culture?

So I ask you to imagine the changes brought on by the queer-parenting phenomenon: infused with love that we send in a healthy direction, held accountable for our actions, committed to the future, forgiving of the past, circumspect and slowed in romance, freed from the yolk of sameness, our hearts on the line as we bring queer children into the queer community. I personally believe that lesbians are some of the most courageous, talented, and honorable people on the planet. We deserve our children, and we should bless them for the changes they are bringing us.

Creating the Night Rainbow
by LauRose Felicity

I have been exposed to many theories about transracial lesbian and gay families. Some urge that black children should not live with white families because they will not learn to be black. And some say that children of color in need of families should be adopted by anyone who will love them—that, first and foremost, children need family. In San Francisco, where I live, black children in need of families outnumber black families seeking them by more than 10 to 1. Some argue that queer people should not adopt children. But some say our experience of "otherness" in American culture gives us special training for preparing children to live and thrive in a climate of bigotry.

After eight years as a mom of children of color I find theories offer food for thought, but no clear guidance. They emerge primarily in response to an urgent wish for *any* explanation that will ease us through (or even around) the arduous passages of life: birth, death, parenting. But they seldom do. Most decisions fall in the spaces between yes and no, requiring understanding of an individual set of experiences, not of a rule applied to a general class.

As a second-generation member of transracial family I find that much of what is said about us comes not from the speaker's experience of similar questions or even from sincere concern. Rather, we simply stir up the speaker's fear of the unknown: We are neither black nor white like him or her; we are some uneasy blend. In the community of my childhood people were horrified by black and white people swimming in the same swimming pools—for a similar reason. If the races played together while scantily clad in a swimming pool, they would "mix."

The making of transracial families (formerly known as "miscegenation: unlawful race mixing") elicits a desperate need for explanation. Like a two-headed calf, the transracial family is considered an uncomfortable anomaly. "What are you?" the biracial child hears on the playground and in government records offices alike. Remember, we are still quite close to a time in America (the 1960s) when transracial families were outlawed. Perhaps the dread that engendered these laws has not vanished, but merely changed shape into scornful social comment.

Why? As with queer folks in general, explanations as to why people love and wish to form family unions with others seldom quiet others' fear of that love. Nonetheless, the desire of people to love each other—over and through racial boundaries—has been and will always be with us. Like sunny yellow dandelions that push triumphantly through the cracks of sweltering city pavements, transracial families spread and flourish.

Given my distaste for general theories of transracial family, I hesitated to write this story. My reticence grew also from too-frequent experiences of unsolicited intrusion into my family. Like a womon whose pregnant belly juts out, a black-plus-white family is viewed as a public spectacle that others feel free to comment upon. A white salesperson at Kmart asked me why my infant was so tan; a black telephone repair woman in my mother's home said her church did not "believe in" transracial adoptions,[1] and lesbians at conferences begin long tirades (pro and con) on the efficacy of our family. A gay man even told me that we only visit the Castro (a queer neighborhood in San Francisco) because we want to flaunt our black children and show that we can "do it" (parent).

Despite the distastefulness of being the object of such derision I agreed to write this article because I think sharing is required to promote better understanding. Moreover, I wanted to lay to rest one especially pernicious train of "thought": that white queer mothers are untouched by their children's experiences of racism. These theorists claim that by sweeping our black children away to the carefree land of "whiteness" we dwell in an endless Indian summer of privilege.

Baloney. In the land of black and white, transracial families are bastards. We get no special protection. Instead, like the white woman's child with a little "color," we are seen as coming from some illicit union. I have previously written of my hunger for lesbian eroticism making me like "an escaped bitch who carries a tainted bloodline," a sexual outlaw. But those of us who leap the fences of race *and* sex frustrate categorization even more. And none of the "theories" about us offer direction in real lives lived outside "normalcy" and at the crossroads of controversy. So what do I write here if I have no theory? Perhaps my experience. Others can then take from it the part that gives them support and disregard the rest.

I also offer a metaphor. Deep in the Cumberland Mountains in Kentucky, where I grew up, stands a visual symbol of a queer transracial family. On some fortunate evenings the rushing falls veil the moonlight in mist. Darkness and light intertwine, and a unique image is born: the night rainbow. Its arch shines in washes of Day-Glo pigment against the deep-purple night sky.

This is the way it is for us. This is the way we are. Never

have we been white mothers and black-and-tan children, distinct from each other as exposures of light and shadow upon a negative. Our herstory, like the spectrum of the night rainbow, is created by the interplay of darkness and light *indivisible*.

At the time of welcoming our children to our family, my partner, Calla, and I made a vow to be family with them forever and to share each joy and challenge that such commitment brings. So as mothers our lives are inextricably interwoven with our daughters' experiences of fortune, black pride, and racism. And, as daughters, our girls live lives that are inextricably interwoven with their mothers' experiences of fortune, light-skin privilege, racial guilt, lesbian pride, and homophobia. As our family stories illustrate, nothing is separable within our intermarriage of light-dark.

Sometimes we describe our palette of skin tones as "tan Mama," "pink Mama," "peach daughter," and "brown daughter." I am tan Mama, but I am also a womon whose light skin conceals dark heritage. I was raised in the segregated South's experience of whiteness *and* blackness in many domains. My mother, Honey, was the companion of a black retired army sergeant for ten years even while she was married to a white lawyer—in a Southern city. I watched her live, eat, drink with, and be held at night by one funny, kind, loving black man while taking dinner—every night for ten years—to her powerful, abusive white husband. My mama's love "across the fence" has indelibly affected the palette of my family's night rainbow.

I learned other lessons of darkness from those whom my family had business and personal relations with. For instance, during all of my childhood my mama rented out clean but modest clapboard houses to black tenants. The caretaker of my father's inheritance, she took her duty seriously to provide habitable housing at affordable rents. My weekends and summers were consumed by scrubbing, painting, papering, repairing, and renting these homes.

Ostensibly, as the property owner, my mother was the "boss" and the one "on top" in any relationships with tenants. But that was not life as we knew it. As a girl I spent many evenings basking in the thick heat inside the living room of Ms. McKinney and her male companion Sweets, as my mother and Sweets snaked out pipes, fixed broken windows, or unclogged a toilet in another house. Like the colored maids in the opposite end of town, my mother did the dirty work her customers needed and paid her for.

Meanwhile, Ms. McKinney, a broad, deeply black womon whose aged feet shuffled her kitchen linoleum in men's shoes cut out to free her bunions, shared not only heat, but life lessons with me. She provided for her family. Her backyard, under her hand, yielded a bumper crop of produce. And she also sold snow cones: frozen treasures glistening with sweet cherry flavor in the breathless Southern summers. Her living-room wall depicted cherished black babies, proud young men in the uniform of our army, and loving partners. These, and the light in Sweets's eyes as he helped Ms. McKinney clear the table, told me of family and love that survived despite the hardships of life in the Jim Crow South.

The relationship of my mother to this aging African-American couple, with their living room full of clean, cheap furniture and images of proud kinfolk, was deep. She never raised their rent, and she didn't demolish their home until after she'd honored them at their funerals. Sweets helped my mother with repairs while she entrusted me to his companion. Life then, as now, was complex and individual, lived across racial boundaries. And, like thieves, we had our own code of honor that was not to be ignored simply because the greater society disdained our bonds.

Tenant-landlord relations, however, were not what affected my family the most. My mother later owned a liquor store in an all-black neighborhood, close to the city's largest housing project. She lived there with Sarge, her lover of more than a decade. Staying with them there, I learned many lessons.

One was about the hierarchy of skin tones and hair textures ("high yallah," best; nappy, worst) that I understood just by watching who was yearned after as they strolled into the bar and ordered their chips and beer. I also learned about parenting: noticed that mothers with pride kept their children's skin from becoming "ashy" (gray from dryness), and oiled and fixed their children's hair daily. Only a "no 'count" mama let her child's braids get nappy. There were also rules of etiquette. Children respected elders by answering "yes, ma'am" and not "yeah" to Mama, Auntie, and Granny. And people called just John or Hattie by white folks were never denied a last name or title by children or friends. So, as I say to my children today, that adult's not "Sue" or "David." That's "Ms. Sue" or "Mr. David" to you.

Most importantly, I learned—even in a climate electrified with black pride and the militancy of those who burned down their own neighborhoods rather than live in a ghetto away from suburban housing they could afford—loyalty rules. I learned some rather dynamic lessons.

As in the film *Do the Right Thing*, our family and our neighbors talked of "prejudice" night and day in the '60s and '70s. But when some participants in a "race riot" shattered and set fire to "white" businesses in our neighborhood, my black neighbors sat on tall stools in my mother's store with shotguns in their laps, guarding her. And, in turn, my mother was the unpaid emissary to countless government bureaucracies because she had the white telephone voice and law office backup. Friends took care of each other. I still live by this, and do not take—or give—trust lightly.

At my mother's store I also learned some notions about family that do not apply to mine. Perhaps because of the open disgust she garnered when appearing in white Louisville society with her longtime black companion, my mother was happy for me when I came out to her as a lesbian, but offered one note of caution: "You may not want to tell everyone." I heard her words, but I had learned the opposite lesson from her life experiences. As my mother had been in a long-term relationship with a black man, in a town where black-white marriage recently had been illegal, the effects of her coping techniques were vivid.

I'd watched as her lover, Sarge, kept his huge hands on the table, ordered another drink, and told uproarious jokes when my dad appeared at the store where Sarge lived with my mother. But I also saw the rage he struggled to check as my father cursed my mother in her business or blackened her eye when her supper delivery had been a few minutes late. And he watched her leave on that supper run every night for ten years. My mother and Sarge were often happy in their own way, but eventually the fear in their life promoted drunken sorrow.

And so my "whiteness" is colored by this experience of blackness in America. I could never live in two worlds as my mother did: white attorney's wife, black man's mistress. So when I came out I told everyone, and vowed to never dishonor a lover by making her a backstreet partner. I knew that lies become habitual and twists those who live with them with fear and resentment.

So now, though our marriage is legitimized only by the simple ceremony of "jumping the broom" that bound our daughters' slave kin together, Calla's and my commitment is our primary reality. We bear the memories of homophobic attacks upon us and of earlier lesbians who were arrested, beaten, and raped because they rejected "sex-appropriate" clothing. But we honor family as Ms. McKinney did—in our work, our children and kin, our galleries of photos, and our sharing of passion and care despite our aging bodies.

So these are some of my family-of-origin experiences, street smarts learned in the interracial university of hard knocks. And they bring me back again to the conviction that family—specifically, interracial family—is created in the interstices: the spaces "between," where theories do not fit. And yet, as shared experience may inform, I offer examples from my present family.

Our older daughter is the peach stripe in our rainbow. Some tell us she could be adoptable as a "passing" child. But that is not the reality of her life; her biracial identity has strongly affected both our life and hers.

Opal was born of a 17-year-old African-American girl. At this time families were jetting to Romania, China, and Korea to secure lighter-skinned babies. But five 14- to 16-year-old girls in the birth mother's class at school were forced to keep the children they wished to place for adoption. As one black family court judge said to me, "You didn't have to fight anyone to get that baby, did you?" He commented on the hundreds of housing projects where toddlers walked about sidewalks and streets unnoticed, and on the thousands of thick foster care files documenting dozens of moves and decades in the lives of children who did not have permanent homes.

Named Opalgaia, "jewel of the mother," by us, our first daughter translates into "hard to place" in the child place-ment industry: not white enough to be white or black enough to be black. (In the town where we lived we knew of one white womon who took her slightly tan adoptive baby to *16* pedia-tricians to determine whether he was part African-American.) But from birth we formed that bond of honor with the child we had searched for. She was our daughter, and we wanted to love and keep her forever. Unfortunately, even as she lay vul-nerable and defenseless in her bassinet, our choice to do so was open to challenge *because* of her blackness.

Before Opalgaia's birth I had family law coworkers (I prac-ticed family law for 22 years, mostly in the area of divorces affected by wife and child abuse) such as one I will call "Nancy," who often quoted the theory that black children should never be placed with white families. Nancy had also become inflamed with homophobia, and had unsuccessfully tried to undermine my job when my spouse worked at my office for a while. Despite the lack of long-term studies of transracial adoptive families to document the accuracy of this "(greater) harm to black children in white families (than in foster-care) theory," Nancy, an African-American attorney and wife of a well-to-do doctor, would have used her beliefs to harm our family. The birth of our daughter gave her this option.

We already had reasons to fear for our family. We were queer in a state that had never approved a lesbian adoption, *and* some would argue that we were "not black enough" to parent our child. We knew Nancy could and would use her connections in the church, the child welfare system, and the community to thwart our adoption. Race would be the alleged issue, but homophobia would be her real agenda for taking our child from the only parents she had.

So we made a painful decision. When Opalgaia was born we told no one but our closest family of her coming to us. Unlike the straight moms who were baby-showered and maternity-leaved, Calla and I worked every day and cared for our infant in secret. Arising the usual four to six times a night to feed her, I attended court the next day without discussing my fatigue. And as I rocked our tiny daughter in her room in our cabin deep in the woods, I held her tight. I was terrified of those who would scream "queer" and "whitey" to steal her from us.

In reality, this light-skinned "black" child had nowhere else to go to but to a succession of foster care homes, where she would be at high risk for physical or sexual abuse, or back home to her birth mother, who did not care for her first child. But a "theory" of "best interests" has been used to keep black children from white parents who bond with and want them, even when black permanent families are not available to take them.

Three home studies and six weeks later our daughter legally became mine. (Joint custody with her comother, Calla, was successfully established later!) And even on that most ecstatic day when we chose to bring our treasured child into the public, a friend shared with me the "truth about your kind of family." An attorney from a respected black family, she proclaimed, "I don't believe in this sort of thing" as I held my daughter in her special adoption dress before her. "These children never fit in anywhere because they aren't white and they won't learn to be black."

Maybe. And maybe they won't learn to be black in a sort of "special" Southern way. Before I left the South I continued every day to carry out groundbreaking civil rights work in the courts and in legal education. I founded a program that helped African-American students take their deserved place of achievement and honor in a historically segregated law school. I made a television documentary that finally recorded the sagas of local African-American elders who had braved injury, insult, and hardship to achieve integration. I successfully had the entire police department held liable for failing to stop the murder of a poor black womon by her children's father. And yet my family and I were invited to the home of only one of my African-American legal colleagues. Exclusion, as a way of policing racial boundaries, prevailed.

But this is where our rainbow pulled together again. We moved from our gorgeous cabin deep in the woods at the end of the road. It was a fantastical place covered in honeysuckle and blackberry vines, tiger lilies, black-eyed Susans, and Queen Anne's lace in the summer. In the winter thick blankets of snow covered it. But black children in our town were physically and emotionally hurt in the local schools. A move to the more urban Louisville followed.

But little actual integration occurred there either. We were banned from lesbian spiritual and social gatherings because we wanted to bring our children. (This "banning" started the year we adopted our second, and very visibly black, child.) We were vehement public advocates for African-American students, victims of domestic violence, and lesbian mothers. But our role was that of an archetype. We were either a scapegoat or a poster family for queer normality. We were seldom seen as "regular" people—in need of friendships and quiet support in our times of joy, sorrow, and daily life. Consequently, we moved to San Francisco, where we have been more fortunate.

To conclude, let me say that the core value most essential to transracial family is absolute loyalty—of each member on the color spectrum to each other, no matter how light or dark. As in queer families, the perceived "queerer" cannot be denied in public or private. Likewise, the blacker family member is the "sweeter juice" ("The darker the berry, the sweeter the juice") to be savored, not disowned.

I have few models for this transracial family code of loyalty. But one I read about deserves mention: the family of the accomplished Delaney sisters. At ages 103 and 105, respectively, in their lifetimes they had served as one of the first black female dentists and the first black schoolteacher in New York. Their parents administered a religious college, and their father was America's first elected black bishop.

The Delaneys' book, *Having Our Say*, speaks mostly of the rich heritage they inherited from their African-American kin.[2] But their European-American relatives deserve and also receive mention. Their grandmother, Miss Martha, was the child of a white man and the grandchild of a white woman who conceived her while her husband was away at war. He adopted the girl and forgave his wife.

Miss Martha loved Mr. Milam, a white man, but they could not marry because of miscegenation laws. He was white, while she was only one-fourth black but seen as "colored" because of the "one-drop" (of colored blood) laws in the South. Nonetheless, she and Mr. Milam were partnered for 50 years. He was devoted to her and made it well-known that "if anyone messed with his 'lady love,' he'd track them down and blow their head off."[3] No one did. Together they amassed a good-size estate and sent their daughter, Nanny, to Saint Augustine's College, and she later used her degree to help thousands of African-American students.

Meanwhile, Mr. Milam also managed to thwart not only the property acts preventing women's rights to control their own wealth, but also the mores inhibiting the property rights of blacks. He left all his and Miss Martha's land and money to their surviving child, Nanny. Thus, the wealth transmitted by this stubborn white man and biracial woman advantaged the Delaney family, helping to bring professional stature and greater ease to at least two generations of accomplished African Americans.

Clearly, as the Delaneys' story illustrates, it is possible for cross-race-boundary loyalty to create lasting change. The night rainbow, indivisible, can be both a fantastic display of color and a multihued bridge from isolation and impoverishment to sharing and unity.

1. This statement cut especially because my youngest daughter, whom she was looking at when she made this comment, was a very at-risk preemie when we met her. Without prenatal care, exposed to disease risks in utero and abandoned in neonatal intensive care, this miracle of a child had to grow to four pounds before we could take her home. Because she'd had to return to the hospital at six weeks of age with pneumonia; had to wear an apnea monitor whose alarms disturbed sleep all night long for three months; and needed to be fed (because of her low weight) every half-hour, I listened with exhaustion to this comment. Called "One Church, One Child," certain programs promote the fostering of a black child by an African-American church. I certainly do not discourage such efforts: Many children, especially those adrift in the foster "care" system for months or years, have *no one* concerned about their well-being. But as the adoptive mother of two African-American children, I wonder why *each* church member doesn't adopt a waiting child rather than a whole

church adopting one. Why also would anyone oppose the creation of a family for a waiting child or criticize those who took on *all* the burdens and joys of an adoptive child?

2. Delaney, B. and Delaney, A.E. with Amy Hill Hearst. *Having Our Say*. New York: Dell Publishing, 1993.

3. Ibid, pg. 45.

First Class: Economics and Queer Families
by Terry Boggis

I direct Center Kids, the family program of the New York Lesbian and Gay Community Services Center and the largest regional LGBT program in the country—and, probably, in the world. Before I directed it, when the program was still run by volunteers, my lover, our son, and I were one of the first families in the program and members of its steering committee since its founding in 1988. I tell you this because, as someone involved with the lesbian and gay parenting grounds on an organizational level—as well as a personal one—for almost nine years, I've had the opportunity to observe a lot.

I get many phone calls (between 50 and 100 a week) from LGBT people needing information on becoming parents and coping with the challenges of parenthood (which are plentiful under the simplest circumstances), with the additional twist of being queer tossed into the mix. These calls, from all kinds of queer people, have taught me a lot over the years. I'd like to share with you some of the things I've learned.

I should say something at the outset: My reflections today have to do with the concept of class, of fitting in, and exclusion.

I know that in this culture, class has many variables: our parents, our parents' parents, our continents and counties of origin, our first languages, our neighborhoods, our tastes, our hairstyles, the things we own, our educations, the possessions and positions to which we aspire, our accents, our pasts, our bloodlines, our accessories. So just to clarify and simplify, when I speak of class here, I'm talking about money.

Over the past 11 years I've watched and participated as we as a group have presented the face of lesbian, gay, bisexual, and (rarely mentioned) transgender parenthood in this country to be white and middle-class. I know differently, though. Queer parents are not only middle-class, educated, comfortable, and employed dual-income guppy couples. We are also people who live in cars with our kids; people who live in rural areas in economically stressed regions with little to look forward to in work or education; lesbian couples who want to have a baby and can't afford to buy sperm; gay men as enthusiastic about the notion of biological parenting as any could be, who can't possibly afford surrogacy arrangements; people who can't imagine affording a camping trip away or a group junket to the circus with other queer families. We are people with AIDS—sometimes with children who also have the virus. Some of us not only can't afford a copy of *Daddy's Roommate* or other books depicting gay families, but the lives reflected in the pages of these books bear no resemblance whatsoever to the lives we lead. We are families on welfare, living in public housing. We are people whose desire to parent is every bit as strong as the middle-class homo, but we lack health insurance sufficient to cover the most basic gynecological care, let alone sperm washing, intrauterine insemination, in vitro, and other sophisticated fertility technologies, or midwifery, or the funds to cover essential legal counsel (a basic requirement in a society in which our children can still be taken away from us).

In my job I hear from lesbian mothers whose pregnancies

have resulted from sex work, drugging, or drinking, or those who have HIV and need to make arrangements for their children while they are working to care for themselves. I hear from young, single lesbians who became pregnant and don't want to be, who seek lesbian or gay parents for adoption placement of their children. In fact, contrary to the popular truism in this community, not all of our families are planned; not all of our children are wanted; not every pregnancy is a carefully planned life transition.

Surrogacy arrangements cost upward of $40,000. International adoptions average $20,000. Private or independent adoptions cost anywhere from $15,000 to $40,000 (and much of that price discrepancy comes from the different values assigned to white children and children of color—a blatant horror). Lesbians, who tend to come to parenting decisions later in life and attempt pregnancy with frozen sperm, encounter infertility problems more often that straight women. Advanced reproductive assistance, such as in vitro fertilization, is very often not covered by health insurance even when a woman is insured.

I recently spoke at a Center Kids support group for gay men and lesbians who were considering parenting biologically. A working-class lesbian couple came to the meeting hoping to meet sperm donors. They had made inquiries at sperm banks and were horrified at the $150-per-shot price quotes, plus assorted adjunct expenses. One of them said, "We just want some sperm!" Her exasperation at their inability to access a substance generally treated as utterly disposable and valueless was enormous. And the men in the room were even more in despair; the costs for them to reproduce (without even getting into the class politics of surrogacy) are even more daunting.

Only men and women of means are able to gain access to the reproductive technologies that allow lesbians and gay men to have children without compromising their sexual identity or health. So what is the upshot of this financial challenge for poor and working-class LGBT people? No surprise: The pathways that remain open include heterosexual contact—anathema to a gay-identified person—or insemination at home with fresh sperm from an unchecked donor, involving health risks that don't come with sperm banks. Do we want to continue to present LGBT parenting as a "sport for the rich, like ballooning or yachting," as a letter writer recently asked in *The New York Times*?

It's interesting to note that through the 30-odd-year-old modern debate on reproductive rights in this country the argument on which we have unswervingly focused is a woman's right to choose abortion. The discourse is invariably cast in the negative: the right not to have a baby. But reproductive rights also means our rights as queer people to reproduce and to have adequate laws in support of alternative family structures to make us feel safe enough to take the risk to parent, to love, and to tend to our kids.

Perhaps more than any other subgroup of this community, ours had been the most vigorous in its assertion that "we're just like everyone else." Who is "everyone else"? What do we envision when we proudly make this pronouncement? We mean white people with money, education, property, and possessions: the American model, the American myth—not true of all of us, and mostly untrue in the larger culture. The desperation for acceptance that lies behind the "we're like everyone else" profession makes me cringe. I understand the impulse behind it; as parents we have a fierce desire for our children to face an unimpeded life, a life without hurt feelings and ostracism for being different. But we're queer, and we are different. Perhaps not in many ways and not in certain ways that really count (i.e., we love our kids, we want what's best for them, we do our best for them as parents, we do homework with them, see to their nutrition and hygiene and health, seek enrichment opportunities, are concerned with their emotional growth, etc.). But still, long after Ellen DeGeneres came out of the closet (not just as a lesbian, but as a really cute Southern California blue-eyed, blond, educated, middle-class lesbian), we are still considered by many to be weird, bizarre, scary, foreign, filthy, untouchable, and uncomfortable to be around.

The point is that being different, being queer, does not make me a bad parent or a good one. I see lesbian and gay parents striving for the "we're better than good, we're weller than well" image, serving as PTA leaders, parent volunteers, cake bakers, the block association leadership, car poolers. All this is fine: indisputably, the more visible we are, the more out, the more prominent, the better. It's what motivates these behaviors that disheartens me. It's that eagerness to please— to prove to people, to whom we don't have to prove anything, that we're just alike and just as good—that kills me. It mimics class striving: that "poor cousin" sort of aping of the prevailing culture, buying the "norm" whole cloth as the only desirable model. I know—I've done it lots of times, and I can feel the tiny deaths inside me each time I try to prove myself worthy of acceptance by straight society when I am so much more nourished and affirmed by making connection with the various members of our wildly diverse queer family.

I actually don't know the answers to the questions I've asked here. I only know that the questions, and the lives that pose them, trouble me. All I know is once again, in a profoundly personal, primal, basic area, it's just not a level playing field. And I know how ironic our situation is: For all time, the one asset, the one abundance that poor people have always had has been children. In the queer community it is our most agonizing area of impoverishment that having children is not always a right we can access.

Where to begin? Given that the current leadership in the LGBT family rights movement identifies as middle-class, how do we move over and share leadership with our working-class families? I think we begin on both the personal and organizational levels by forming alliances with other progressive people and movements: welfare rights, immigration rights, reproductive rights, labor rights. I think we begin by claiming all members of the LGBT parenting community as our closet kin rather than striving to claim alliance with and allegiance to Ward and June Cleaver. Then we can display our unique competencies as parents not just like everyone else, but of our own kind of ideal.

Lesbian, Gay, and Transgender Parents Creating Family Together:
When the Best Laid Plans Run Amok
by Marcia Perlstein and James Hughson

We're a community often under siege for loving whom we love and creating the family units we create. Everything from hate crimes to adverse legislation demands our energy, financial resources, and time. Yet in spite of those who would prefer that we didn't exist, we are envisioning and creating the nurturing units we desire. I've had more difficulty than usual in getting my part of this article written. Jim, my coauthor, completed his section immediately, and I procrastinated so long that I had to turn my therapist lens onto myself. I realized I have a good deal of secondary trauma for all the pain I continue to when loving arrangements fall apart. Rapidly approaching deadline…faces of anguished mothers, fathers, children flashed across the screen of my mind…making it difficult to focus on the computer screen.

First and foremost, we would like to acknowledge the beauty, creativity, and excitement of the "gayby boom" and the alternative family movement. Without legal sanctions many

LGBT adults have been able to bring children into their homes and hearts, providing functional, nurturing units. We now have an abundance of services, Web sites, and publications. We have support groups, potlucks, networks, and serious scholarship devoted to the study of what we are creating. We are slowly developing legislation to support the families we are creating and are persevering despite numerous setbacks. Our greatest strides so far have been in the area of adoption. Legally, the dark side is that we've still lost far too many custody battles for no reason other than being gay.

Many of the simple things that families headed by heterosexual couples take for granted are denied us, so we fight for recognition of our basic rights. We know our families are no more functional or dysfunctional than those created by our outwardly more traditional counterparts. Much has been written about this, even in the popular media. What we have been more reluctant to focus on, because of some serious threats from outside our LGBT community, are the internal shadows in our families, the problems we encounter in learning to live in the families we have created. Some of the issues faced by our families are similar to our counterparts; others are unique to families with LGBT members. The latter will be our focus. We plan to look at the roots of some of the problems that arise when gay men and lesbians come together to parent, then talk about ways that we at the Alternative Family Project try to help families soften or even reverse some of the negative impact.

Once again, this difficult examination is done from a foundation of homage to the courage and joy that is also part and parcel of the gayby boom. We'd also like to take this opportunity to acknowledge as well the large cadre of straight allies who walk the walk side by side with us.

Overview

The majority of difficulties occur because—no matter how

much people prepare in advance for the scenario they imagine that they wish to live—inevitably the unexpected occurs. Emotions are stirred up; sometimes folks can handle these situations themselves, but often outside interventions are needed by a therapist or mediator. Sadly, the child often gets lost in the fray as adults may have the genuine intention of serving "the best interests of the child," but primitive emotions are triggered that they may have difficulty controlling and understanding.

We often have no guideposts or precedents to turn to. The families we are creating are truly works in progress. In this article we'll view some situations from the vantage point of the larger issues they represent. All the examples included have been changed, mixed, and blended to protect the anonymity of those involved.

Alternative Family Project

Started by a lesbian mom in 1993 who found that services weren't available for her family, AFP helps folks in the LGBT community create families and learn to live in them. To help us serve as many families as possible we have an active intern program in which we train LGBT counseling interns at all stages of their professional process and, most importantly, who have the heart and soul of service and seek to be firmly grounded in our community. We offer support groups for parents, prospective parents, and children; counseling for couples, family and children; celebration; and information and advocacy. We have tried to help sparring families avoid the legal system, but where we find our clients being treated homophobically we have stepped in as advocates and, working with attorneys in many cases, we support our clients' efforts to retain or regain custody of their children. Our strongest thrust is in the area of preventing legal conflicts, helping LGBT coparents come together with as much clarity and goodwill as possible in planning ways to create family. We also have held a variety of community forums to learn about and discuss complex issues, such as the options and avenues of parenthood as well as legal issues in same-sex relationships. We have a healthy appreciation for the range and variety of issues that arise, and know that solutions must be customized to suit all parties involved. And the sad truth is that, despite all our experience and good intentions, there are some families who come to us late in the process of deterioration and for whom we are not able to help find resolution.

First- and Second-Story Emotions

First, a couple of definitions. First-story emotions are those directly related to the issue. Second-story emotions arise when overlays of negative intention get added to the mix. In these cases second-story emotions express themselves when at least one person feels other adults in the picture are being treated poorly on purpose. Most of the time, when outside intervention is sought, the situation has progressed to out-of-control, second-story emotions.

Scenarios and Discussion

Triangles

David, Ann, and Julia talked for several months about how they wanted to raise their child and what roles they would each play. They even wrote their agreements in the form of a contract. They had met at a group for gays and lesbians who were considering parenthood, and they wanted to raise their child in a three-parent household. Ann and Julia are partners, but they wanted all three people to be equal parents. They went so far as to jointly buy a duplex house. That way, David could live separately from Ann and Julia, but the child would have access to all three parents. They would have separate private lives but would live under one roof.

Ann was impregnated with David's sperm, and the pregnancy went well, but rifts in the relationships began to appear.

Julia started to feel like a third wheel—that she was not a part of the bond between the biological mother and father. When the baby was born, Ann and Julia asked David not to be in the birthing room, in order to give Julia a chance to bond with the baby. David was disappointed, but he agreed.

After the baby was born, Ann and Julia were concerned about leaving the infant alone with David in his part of the house. David felt like his access to the baby was severely constrained even though he was still expected to contribute his full amount of financial responsibility and time for household chores. Julia still felt left out of the parental bond and became concerned that she had no legal parental rights. Ann and Julia asked David if he would be willing to give up his paternal rights. He was not. David felt like he was being squeezed out of the relationship.

Now their relationships are strained to the breaking point. At home they barely speak to each other. All three are in counseling together, but too often the counseling sessions turn into shouting matches. This is far from the relationship they had envisioned.

Discussion

The above is, unhappily, more common in our community than we would wish. The contract Ann, Julie, and David made didn't fit the eventual situation. Triangles are common when three people are involved, and often there are shifting alliances. The non-birth parent initially felt isolated; now the dad is being shut out by the moms. For the foreseeable future the alliances will probably remain static rather than shifting. They found themselves unable to play out the "dream of equality" in real life. Due to their shifting alliances none of the adults feel they have equal access to the child. These are basic issues of inclusion, which is essential to any system with three adults. If not, the situation is not resolved; the child may eventually learn to play the adults against each other. Hopefully they will come to a pre–legal-system resolution that will involve acceptance of shifts and each of the adults learning to form a relationship with the child based on their own unique set of strengths and interests to be shared with the child.

Their therapy might progress in the direction of planning for shifts rather than their feeling betrayed by the inevitable changes that occur. Right now their wounds are too deep for this to occur quickly; they need to understand each other's pain in a genuine way so they can stop hurting each other over and over and let the healing begin.

Someone Changes Her/His Mind

Ken and Dana, both in their early 40s, have been friends since college. Ken owns a plumbing business in San Francisco, and Dana is a freelance writer who divides her time between San Francisco and Hawaii. When they decided to have a child together Ken thought he would like the role of uncle. Dana would have complete decision-making and parenting responsibilities, and Ken would be a frequent visitor when Dana and the child were in San Francisco. They decided that when the child was five Dana would settle in the Bay Area.

Ken bonded with the infant the first time he saw the baby: right after the birth, which took place in Hawaii. Ken was astounded by the strength of his feelings. He had to return to his business in San Francisco and would not see the baby for several months, which frustrates him. Then Ken will be able to see the baby for only six months out of the year for the next five years. Ken wants to play a more integral role in the baby's life, but that conflicts with the agreement Ken and Dana made. He does not know what to do now.

Discussion

Ken is doing something important that hopefully will prevent this situation from deteriorating further. He is using his own individual therapy and participation in a gay men's group to get support for his feelings. He is not trying to change the arrangement. Hopefully Ken can see the cup as half full by focusing on his time with the baby rather than his time apart from the child. Perhaps if he lets go a bit and enjoys the time he has, Dana will feel less threatened about changing plans and will welcome more and more participation from him. It also is not written in stone that the geographic separation will remain for as long as initially envisioned. When one party wants to change the plan, s/he needs to understand that pushing or throwing weight around will only provoke countervailing force in response. If Diana does not welcome his involvement further down the road, Ken can consider other options for asking Dana to participate in changing the arrangements. There is a great expanse between the extremes of doing nothing and getting into ugly and costly custody battles.

It should be noted that when gay men and lesbians do get into court, the men often have a greater economic advantage, just as straight men do in our culture. The consequences include distrust between lesbians and gay men; children losing time with their mothers (or in worst-case scenarios, mothers losing custody of their children); a time and energy drain for everyone involved; and situations in which women, in greater numbers than men, cannot sustain prolonged court battles and thus suffer unfavorable outcomes.

Children Acting Out Adults' Tension

Beth and Kathy have been together five years. Beth has a nine-year-old daughter from a previous heterosexual marriage. Both have jobs, but Kathy provides most of their financial support. For the past year the daughter, Vivian, has been acting out by yelling at and hitting her classmates at school.

About two years ago Vivian's father, Michael (who had left when he and Beth divorced), reappeared. Vivian was two at the time, and Michael has had only sporadic contact with Beth and Vivian since then. Now he is talking about wanting more visitation rights.

Kathy feels caught in the middle. She does not know how much of a disciplinarian she should be with Vivian. She wants to discuss parental roles with her partner, but Beth feels overwhelmed by the problems with both Vivian and Michael, and does not have the energy to deal with Kathy's anxieties too. Kathy wonders how long she can stay in the relationship if things remain the same. Beth and Kathy are both afraid Michael could cause even bigger problems if he insists on partial custody.

Discussion

These are standard blended-family issues as well as those of unresolved grief and abandonment. Often children act out the tension they perceive around them. If Beth could let Kathy in as more of an ally than an additional problem, Vivian might get some of the stability she lost when her father pulled out of her life, and Kathy might get some of the benefits of stepparenting, along with its responsibilities and travails. As a unit Beth and Kathy might have greater strength to deal with Michael. The mere threat of a custody battle is wreaking havoc with this family. Beth needs to help Vivian deal with the early loss of her father and to find out what her needs are. Stepparents are often given mixed messages about what is wanted and expected of them.

The road can be a bit bumpy while the two mothers work it out. Every situation is different, but the process needs to be a negotiation rather than a unilateral decision. Beth is probably a bit scared to share parental control with Kathy just at a time when she really needs to share. The additional stress of not knowing whether Vivian's father will return makes it even more important that the moms resolve some of these issues.

Since everyone is in such a tizzy Vivian is getting a bit lost in the fray. The only way she knows to indicate this is by acting out rather than speaking her pain. The adults in her life need to lead the way. Beth, Kathy, and Vivian are all in family therapy. Vivian gets some of her own special time within these sessions in play therapy with the family therapist. The moms are learning how to work with her feelings. Then they all can look toward their various options with Michael. He needs their help in understanding the impact of his comings and goings before any choices can be made.

Dissolution of Relationship: Nonbiological Parent Deprived of Parental Rights

Pat and Jerry were a couple for four years. After they were together for a year they decided to have a child. Jerry is a female-to-male transgendered person, so they used an unknown donor for Pat to become pregnant. Their son, Billy, has grown up thinking of Jerry as "Dad" even though Pat and Jerry had never legally married.

Two years ago Pat and Jerry separated, and the process was hard on both of them; Pat wanted to end the relationship, but Jerry wanted to stay together. Although Billy stayed with Pat, they decided Jerry would visit frequently. Sometimes they would share a meal together, and other times he and Billy would go somewhere for the afternoon.

Six months ago Pat and Billy moved in with Pat's new partner, Mary Anne. There is some tension between Jerry and Mary Anne, but Jerry has expressed a desire to continue seeing Billy, who is now five. Billy has become slightly withdrawn since he and Pat moved in with Mary Anne. Mary Anne and Pat think that the number of adults in Billy's life is confusing him, and they want him to think of Mary Anne as his other parent. Consequently, they have told Jerry that he can no longer visit.

Jerry is distraught and does not know what to do or where to turn for help. He has discovered that he has no legal rights, since he did not adopt Billy, but he feels that even if he had, the courts would rule against him because he is transgendered.

Discussion

This is the single biggest shadow in our community, wreaking havoc for kids and parents alike. In divorce or dissolution, the nonbiological parent is often forced out of the child's life, having no legal protection from the acted-out wrath of the biological parent. Transphobia is even more vicious than homophobia in these cases. A nonbiological, or even biological, transgender parent, must fight in discriminatory situations time after time, often with little support to prevent themselves from being cast out of their children's lives. At AFP our Transgender Parents group is one of the few places folks can offer each other both practical assistance and emotional support.

When Adults Work as a Team: Children's Inevitable Confusions Worked Through

Nine years ago Jim, who was 28 at the time, impregnated a bisexual friend of his during an evening when they were celebrating his friend's new job. His friend did not want to have a child at that point in her life and was going to have an abortion, but after much discussion Jim convinced her that he both wanted and would be able to raise the child. Since he worked from home as a software developer he felt he would be able to attend to the baby's needs. After the baby's birth he also received some welcome assistance from his mother, who lived in a nearby town. She stayed with him for the first two months that he had the baby, then helped him out periodically.

When the boy, Scott, was three, Jim and Peter became life partners. Jim and Peter began sharing parental responsibilities, and Scott called Jim "Daddy Jim" and Peter "Daddy Peter." Sometimes Scott dropped the "Daddy" and just used their first names.

Peter and Scott had just returned from a visit to Peter's parents, where they had stayed for a few days and had been part of a family get-together. Jim was unable to attend because he was working on a project with an imminent deadline. During the visit a relative who was looking for Peter had asked Scott, "Where's your father?"

Scott looked puzzled, and the relative repeated, "Peter, where is he?"

"Oh," said Scott, "he's not my real father. My real father is at home."

Peter overheard this exchange and felt stung but thought that it would be better to deal with it later. After they returned home Peter told Jim about the incident when they had some time alone. After some discussion they decided that the best way to handle it would be for Jim to talk to Scott privately.

The next day Jim took Scott for ice cream. Jim told Scott that Peter had heard him say that Peter was not his real father, so Jim wanted to talk about what a father was. Jim asked Scott to give some examples of what a father does. For the examples that Scott gave, such as tucking him in at night and playing ball with him, Jim noted that both he and Peter did that. For some of the examples, Jim did them most of the time, and for other examples Peter did. Suddenly Scott's eyes widened. "O-o-oh," he said. "I bet I made him feel bad." Jim agreed that he might have and also indicated that it was easy to get confused since Peter came into Scott's life later than Jim.

Scott finished his ice cream in silence, and when they returned home Scott rushed to Peter, threw his arms around him, and said, "You're my daddy too!"

Discussion

Sometimes, in their efforts to understand roles and relationships, children inadvertently hurt the adults who are trying to move into parental roles. In a textbook case for unobtrusive exploration, these gay dads worked out a sticky situation. It helped that the fathers were noncompetitive and that the mother followed through on her original plan to turn the child rearing over to the biological father. Jim is prepared to welcome Scott's mom into his life at any point she changes her mind but would retain, with Peter, primary responsibility for raising Scott. Jim and Peter problem-solve as a unit, and rather than pressure Scott to accept Peter, they try to respond to situations that allow Scott to become less confused and more able to see labels such as *father* in expansive rather than restrictive terms. They both knew that Scott considered Peter a father in all the ways that mattered most and were able to build upon that knowledge.

Last Words

The real last words are that there are none: No two issues are exactly alike. There are countless examples of other adult roles, such as that of aunts, uncles, grandparents, etc. Gay/Lesbian Outreach to Elders (GLOE) and AFP launched a grandparent program three years ago that affords older members of our community—who thought, when they came out in their teens and 20s, they had to be childless—ways to remain true to themselves and still have children in their lives. So for every horror story told in detail in this article and the countless others intimated at, there are dozens of examples of collaboration, compromise, and gratification on the steepest emotional and spiritual levels.

May we continue as a community to dialogue and learn, to put our hearts and minds together in creating and growing functional families that fly in the face of naysayers. Let's put the Newts and Pats on notice that they cannot co-opt the term *family*. For we are family, and there are more that work well than those that don't.

Our thanks to Marcia's consultation group: Marny Hall, the late Jean Adelman, and Lu Chaikin; our intrepid editor, Jess

Wells; and Alternative Family Project's interns. National Center for Lesbian Rights has always responded to AFP's calls for information as well as legal advocacy. We have a number of clients in common and feel that when each organization brings its special skills to the mix, clients are better served. Our very special thanks to Kate Kendell and the entire staff at NCLR.

No Place Like Home
by Arlene Istar Lev

"Becoming black is an inside job.... [My son's] evolution into a proud black man will occur largely outside the walls of our home...well beyond the reach of my loving white arms." —Jana Wolff

We are rushing through the mall when we are suddenly aware we are being watched. My partner leans into me slightly, whispering innocently, "Why are these people staring at us?" I catch a glimpse of our family in the mirrored sides of the escalator. In the reflection I see my handsome, red-haired, butch partner wheeling the stroller while our chubby-faced, brown-skinned son is joyfully singing; I stand beside them, my red nails catching the glaring fluorescent lights and bouncing like streaks of lightning back at us in the mirror. The heat and shock of this electric current hits me with all the force of a thunderstorm. My family, my precious, sweet family—the only home I've ever known—stands out awkwardly, noticeably. We are somehow "odd," different, and only barely welcome in the malls of America; our queerness presents a dissonant picture to the suburban shoppers.

That we are different, queer, is not exactly news to us. (On some level, I would worry far more if I "fit in" at the mall without raising an eyebrow.) I jibe in this world as an out Jew and a lesbian. I have been a hippie and a braless feminist—I am sure that if I were younger, I would be pierced like a kewpie doll—I have lived the pain and joy of otherness. My partner and I walk in this world with round, fat bodies, and the erotic nature of our relationship is visible to all. Our queerness has never been secret.

But there is a different danger now as strangers' eyes pierce my son's glowing laughter, annihilating his presence with what looks like disgust. I cannot minimize this hatred in a world where lesbian families are teargassed at the San Diego Pride parade (a pregnant woman and three-year-old hospitalized) with nary a peep from the national media. I cannot ignore this ignorant evil in my neighborhood, where the slightest suggestion of a three-year-old temper tantrum in a tall black child is viewed as threatening. My black son's life is worth diddly-squat, precisely because his most vulnerable behavior is viewed as potentially menacing. My family is a danger to the American way of life, and therefore my family is in grave danger.

❖ ❖ ❖

I am on the phone with my mother, discussing with her the possibility of adoption. She suggests I adopt an Asian child. "They're almost white," she says. I'm baffled by this bizarre racist statement, but I have since heard it many times. She says unequivocally, "You wouldn't adopt a black child, would you?" Her voice gets hard on the word "black." It's a dirty word, and she knows it, but she isn't going to flinch from its nastiness. With my stomach in my chest I say, "Well, I would certainly consider it."

She pauses and calculates as if attempting to be rational with someone who is clearly mentally ill. She tells me about a TV program she saw that showed how black children raised by

white parents grow up to hate them. I try to explain that chil-
dren get angry with their parents for many reasons (knowing she
would miss the irony of this conversation). I tell her that many
white parents do not raise their black children within the con-
text of their own culture; parents often try to deny their chil-
dren's ethnicity, which is why they become upset. My mother
says, "They are so angry," slurring the word "they." "They have a
lot to be angry about," I say, stressing the word "they." She says,
"Sure they do! But why have them mad at YOU?"

Indeed, my mother's racism was not simply about the color
of the child's skin. It wasn't a principled racism based on natural law or racial superiority. My mother's concern was for me,
a white woman with white privilege who could easily adopt
another child, a whiter child, and not open myself up to either
black or white rage. A black person is a target in this culture,
and she just didn't want to stand too close to that karma.

I was a single lesbian when I adopted my one-week-old son.
After many years of struggling with infertility, I had just made
an appointment for the following week to speak to an in vitro
specialist. A friend called to tell me that her lover's sister had
just given birth to a baby boy, whom she was giving up for
adoption. This is what she told me: "His mother just doesn't
want him, and we simply can't take in another child. [They
had three.] He's just lying there in the nursery. Every other
baby has family members gathering around and ogling their
babies, and he's alone in the corner. His name tag says 'Baby
Boy.' His mother will sign the final papers to relinquish him to
the state tomorrow. Do you want him?"

I remember saying "yes" on my out breath. I do not remember thinking about my mother's reaction. I do not remember
thinking about having a son versus having a daughter. I do not
remember thinking about the politics or risks of adoption. I do
not remember thinking *Why me? Why did you call me?* I do
not remember thinking about race. I only had one thought,

which was half formed: *baby*. As the thought matured over the next few minutes, it became *a baby*, and then *my baby*, and then it just turned over and over inside me like warm clothes in the dryer, tumbling around: *my baby, my baby.*

"Yes! Yes! Of course I want him. When can I get him? What should I do?" I waited through that long weekend. I worried that his birth mother would change her mind. I worried about how I was going to find a baby-sitter so I could go to work on Tuesday. My life had a surreal feeling, as I knew that everything was going to change, yet everything seemed so incredibly usual. Everyone told me to sleep because I might never sleep again, but of course I couldn't. I went out to Ames and bought $500 worth of baby things, including the most expensive car seat, one bib, and two bottles.

The phone call came on the first night of Sukkoth, the Jewish harvest festival, and my son came home on Simchas Torah, the day in Jewish tradition that God gave Moses the Torah, our most holy book. Monday morning arrived, and they piled out of the car: three black women, four black children (I briefly worried about car seats), and one rather smelly, large, wide-eyed black baby.

His birth mother handed me this precious, holy baby, they piled back into the car, and I became a mother.

I did not realize the earthquake of changes that transracial queer adoption would unleash. I did not realize when I offered to take in a homeless baby that I too would become homeless. I expected resistance to the adoption from certain communities. I expected homophobia from the patriarchal, heterosexist mainstream community that considered gay parenthood anathema. I also knew that many lesbian and gay parents felt unsupported within the gay community and that parenting would change my relationship to my lesbian community. I suspected that the Jewish community would struggle with accepting a child of color and that the issue of adoption, particularly transracial adoption, would raise issues for many people, including my family. Finally, I expected resistance from both white supremacists and black nationalists, whom I knew would find my family's very existence offensive.

I had, however, lived my rather queer life in a mixed-race and alternative Jewish community, and many of my close friends were parents. I naively thought that within the confines of my alternative lifestyle my family would be bell-curve normatively queer. But I was not prepared for the multiple levels of issues transracial queer adoption would raise, even for the most progressive of my friends.

Even after 25 years of antiracism activism I did not realize how much white privilege I had until it was revoked. Being the mother of a black child meant I was no longer fully a member of the white privileged elite even if I had wanted to be. I no longer had the choice of moving within white culture as if it were my own. I was marked as a "nigger lover," as my mother had warned me I would be. Being the white mother of a black child is not the same as being the white lover of a black man or even a black woman. I do not want to minimize the racism levied at interracial couples, especially interracial queer couples, but in my experiences, it does not compare to the discomfort raised by transracial parenting. Even people who are uncomfortable with interracial adult relationships believe it to be an "adult" decision. The idea of transracial parenting, particularly queer transracial parenting, raises concerns for the child: the unwilling participant in perceived deviance. As if other children are lucky enough to choose their parents and upbringing.

I was so delirious with joy those first few weeks that I didn't notice that my white friends kept asking me if I could "handle this." Yes, they admired the baby as all babies are admired—toes tickled and tushies squeezed—but they also had worried looks. They worried about me being a single parent and they worried about the cost of adoption and they worried if his birth mom would or could take him away—all honest concerns but not quite the whole truth. Like all new mothers, I was too busy in the beginning to take much notice, but over time I realized they seemed to spend a lot of time discussing his skin color, which darkened as the days passed. I began to realize they were uncomfortable, a bit awkward, with his racial features, which would come out as mild jokes about his wide nose or thick lower lip. The teasing was lighthearted and loving, not different from how other children might be teased for their baldness or having Uncle Henry's big nose, but it became tedious. They were struggling to integrate his blackness into their lives, as was I.

Flipping through the pictures of my three-week-old son, I come upon one shot taken at a bad angle, looking right up his nose. His nostrils look so wide, I freeze looking at the picture. Who is this child? Could this be "my" child? How could I be the parent of someone with such different features than mine?

Racism, for most of my white friends—perhaps for most white people—is something "out there," something they witness from the comfort of their living rooms: watching a Klan rally on television or reading a newspaper article about poverty in black ghettos. They cluck their tongues and shake their hands and switch the station, or turn the page, to something less stressful. They view themselves as nonracist and abhor racist laws and police violence. They explain the fact that all their friends are white as a random toss of the dice. They do not see themselves as participants in racist behavior, but as someone above or outside it. This, of course, veils their own racism and ignorance, and absolves them of any daily responsibility in the perpetuation of the racist system.

In the first two years of my son's life, white friends, white neighbors, white colleagues, white baby-sitters, and white day care workers told me again and again how soft his hair felt. His hair is a lovely, nappy brown. It is not particularly coarse, but is certainly not "soft," especially by white standards. But they would pat him on the head, like a cute puppy, and tell me how soft his hair was. I have never had a black person do this. I began to wonder if these white people never touched African woolly hair before. Did they think it was wiry like a Brillo pad? Certainly they were more comfortable touching him as a baby than they could have been touching black adults.

A Latina friend said she taught her daughter to never let anyone touch her hair. She said this with a vehemence that shocked me at the time. It seemed so intense, a way to further separate the races to the point that white people could never know what other races' hair felt like, which I thought would just increase white ignorance. Moreover, it seemed cruel to me to have this pretty little girl child, with her hair so lovingly braided, never being touched. I wanted to be able to touch her head casually with ease as I would touch any child's head or hair.

I have come to understand that her hair is off-limits for touch as my body is off-limits. Not because I am ashamed of my body or because touch does not feel good but because I can't trust others, except those to whom I am very close, to respect my body; it is better to not be touched than to be touched in a way that is not sacred.

White supremacy is not only ubiquitous, but also insidious. When white people see me on the streets, they are often overly enthusiastic, ardent in their desire to recognize and honor this black child in a white woman's arms. They always assume he is adopted. They never assume I have given birth to him. They always assume he has been adopted from the social service system. They often say, "He is so lucky." They assume I have saved him from some horribly abusive situation and that he is now in a white home where he will be safe.

Sometimes black women have said this too—usually older women, grandmothers. They check me out and look deep in my eyes; they are testing me to see if I am capable of the task. If I pass their scrutiny, their words and actions seem to convey a sense of relief, as if to say, "This one will have it easier."

I suppose it is true that if I did not adopt my son, he would have been placed in the system. Perhaps he would have been in many foster homes, perhaps he would have become another victim of the system. His biological mother has lost custody of her two other children, and there is no doubt in anyone's mind, including his biological grandmother and aunt, that he has a better life now than he could have had if he had not been placed for adoption. It is, however, hard for me to see how I saved him when it is so clear that he has saved me. His biological mother did not know she was pregnant; she thought she had miscarried. It has been suggested that perhaps there had been twins. I hold a vision of my embryonic son crawled up inside his birth mom, hiding and totally quiet so no one would know he was there. Both Jews and blacks know a lot about hiding; our ancestors have excelled at it—in barns and on rivers, in the woods and in attics. We hide for our survival.

I have always viewed my son's existence in my life as a gift from the gods, undeserved in some way; I am relieved they finally decided to recognize me and respond to my prayers. His name, Shaiyah Ben Lev, in Hebrew means "God's gift, son of the heart," and "shade" or "protection" in Sanskrit. As a tree offers shade and protection to those who stand beneath it, my son—God's most precious gift to me—protects me from my barren womb and from a life without children's laughter. I did not save him; he saved me.

I am bringing my son in public for his first outing on a cold winter's day, and I notice some black friends talking in the aisle of the concert hall. They do not come over to the baby and me, but keep glancing toward the baby carriage. I take a deep breath and carry my round, warm bundle over to them. "Would you like to see him?" I ask, proud as a peacock. I attempt to ignore their obviously cool stares. "Sure," they lie, and barely looking at my handsome son, they nod and say, "Very nice."

They turn away, excluding us from their circle.

I must admit, I didn't expect this. I did expect blatant racism from the white community and less blatant racism from the Jewish community. I did expect raw honesty and abject ignorance from my immediate family. I did expect cold stares from both white and black strangers on the streets. In my ignorance, though, I did not expect negative reactions from within my own community and from my friends of color.

I am having lunch with a friend, and today she is very angry. She is angry because, in her words, "Things are getting worse all the time for people of color." I am surprised to hear her say this. Not because I am ignorant of how bad things are for people of color, but because I do not agree that things are getting worse. "Are they worse than they were a little more than 100 years ago before slavery was abolished?" I ask. I am clearly making her furious. "I am talking about the poverty in our community," she says, clearly not including me in "our," though she is far wealthier than I will ever be. I remember reading the other day in Essence *magazine that the numbers of black women opening their own businesses is extraordinarily high, and I report this success. My friend looks away from me, disgusted. "How many of those businesses fail?" she asks.*

I am disheartened and clearly losing ground by the minute. I am not new to the righteousness of black anger, but it is true that I am not used to having it turned on me. Black friends have often shared with me their frustration at other white people. Only half jesting, they will say to me, "What is with you people?" but their tone tells me they know that "we" are not all the same. My friends' anger does not scare me, but I do feel sick to my stomach. There's something here I am not getting. I am not sure how we came to be on different teams. We are suddenly not two radical lesbian-feminist antiracism activists battling a racist patriarchy—we are white and black, and the fence between us is insurmountable. My friend looks at me, glaring, and says,

"You have to believe things are getting better because you're raising a black son."

I am deflated, my white flag waving in the breeze.

She is right, of course. I am raising a black son in a war zone. I was warned by more than one African-American mom: "They are only considered cute until six or seven. Then they're in trouble." Do I have to believe things are getting better because I cannot believe my son is truly in the grave danger he is in? How can I rise up to what is being asked of me? My friend accepts that the danger her children are in is a given, but my white-skin privilege means I have lived all my life with racism as something "out there," not something directed at my child. I will never have the skills my friend has to recognize, prepare for, and combat racism—not if I read all the books and go to all the right meetings and wear my "Practice Antiracism" buttons. I was born to this world with shiny white privilege *even* as a Jew, *even* having been raised a working-class girl, *even* as a dyke. I parent my son as all Jewish mothers have. I expect him to survive and thrive. I am not ignorant to racist violence or the social cost of blackness. Blackness, though, evokes a different kind of bigotry than the invisible oppressions I have experienced. I have learned to survive anti-Semitism, classism, and homophobia, to a large extent, by ignoring them. Although my roots are always showing, of course, I do not walk in the world with my Jewishness, my working-class background, or my lesbianism visible in the way blackness is visible. Although I never purposely pass, I have unconsciously used my invisibility as a survival tool. Not only is this a tool my son will not be able to utilize, but also one that will be used as a weapon against him.

A white woman, the mother of three African-American children, tells me this story: They are walking out of a grocery store, and a white male employee glares at her teenage children, then loudly slurs a racial epithet. She says her first reaction is to give him a big piece of her mind. Instead she stops, noticing her children are watching her to see what she will do. She realizes she cannot mimic this kind of aggressive, confrontational behavior. She cannot teach her child to respond to white violence with more violence. She marches up to the manager on duty and explains the situation. They go home and write a letter to the store owner. Her children watch her every move, learning how to protect themselves without endangering themselves. I wonder if I would have held my tongue, if I would have remembered to put the tools in the tool kit that will serve my child.

An African-American friend says to me, "The problem with you white parents is you think you can protect your black children from racism." I do not answer her, but spend the next year contemplating this statement.

Here is my answer: I do want to protect my son from racism. What parent would not want to protect their children from becoming fodder for an angry white policeman's frustrations or an elementary schoolteacher's prejudice? I also want to protect my child from schoolyard bullies and fast-moving cars, from electric outlets and large bodies of water. I want to protect him as well from poverty and homophobia and anti-Jewish hatred. What parent would not want to do the same? The sad truth is that neither of us can protect our children from the ravages and pain of the world.

People of color have good reasons to be concerned about white adoption of "their" children. They have good reasons to be concerned that white families will not only be ill-equipped to teach them how to survive racism, but, more importantly, that they will not be able to cultivate pride in their unique culture and heritage. How would I feel if Jewish children were being raised in Hindu or Catholic homes, albeit good and loving homes? Would I believe they were able to sing the right songs, eat the right foods, and learn the rhythm of our ways of life? I admit I would be leery, doubtful that a non-Jewish family could pull this off and have a child with a sense of comfort and pride in his identity.

Black friends are right to question whether I am up to the task. My issue is that they don't ask. They have not engaged me in conversations about adoption or race or even mother-hood. What they have done is shut me out. Friendly lunches became unanswered phone calls. Invitations to dinner are not returned. I hear through the grapevine that they don't want to be used as a "role model" for my son. My son at the time was not yet crawling and was a long way from noticing the racial configurations of those who came and went in our home. How did my measure of these friendships come down to race? The only role models I have wanted for my son were those I would have wanted anyway. If I had birthed my son or if he were white-skinned, wouldn't I still want my black friends to be his role models? The sad part is that my son has lost good role models—and, indeed, good black role models—and we are all the worse for that. The majority of African-American children available for adoption today are victims of a long history of racism in this country. They are victims of a system that has placed thousands of African-American children in foster care and has not created the economic support within the black community to foster them. That black children can and should be raised within their own communities is, to me, obvi-ous. That the African-American community should be furious at the racist system that destroys its families is also obvious. However, the rejection by African-American activists of black children being raised in white homes is unconscionable. It may be difficult, given the history of racism and all the prob-lems with the system, to expect black families to embrace white families who are raising black children. It may be too much to ask black families to extend the arms of their cultur-al matrix to include all their black children being raised in white homes. The reality, however, is that many black children are being raised in white homes, and to turn their backs on these families is to condemn African-American children to the very white-bread existence that they feared for these children.

I decide to confront a friend. I say, "You've been avoiding me since the adoption. It's obvious you have feelings about this. Can we talk about it?"

She shakes her head and says, "It is done."

It is said as pronouncement, as one might announce the sex of a newborn child ("It's a boy") or a doctor might report the loss of a patient ("I'm sorry, but your father has died"). It is irrefutable and not open to discussion. It is a fait accompli, a done deal. Irrevocable, undeniable, and something she will have to accept with the grace of all survivors who must accept the unacceptable. It is done.

When the coldness of the Christian world becomes too much, as a Jew I can always "go home." It's true, as I am an out lesbian, that not every Jewish space is warmly welcoming to me, but many are. There are many places—shuls and community centers—where I can go and just sit and hear the familiar refrains of davenen or the high-pitched gossip of older women gathering in the kitchen to prepare sweet desserts and weak coffee. I can close my eyes and breathe the smells and shuckle to the comfortable rhythm of what is most familiar.

I walk into Leo's bakery, where Friday afternoons are crowded with Jews preparing for the Sabbath. Most shoppers are not religious; this is for them a secular event, a way of marking time and reserving space for their families. Whether or not you are known by name, everyone chats with each other, sticking their noses a bit too closely into each other's bakery goods, wondering aloud if the bobka is as good as the German coffee cake and if Aunt Sylvia would like it better.

I am holding my new son in my arms. I am still new to carrying a newborn baby and am endlessly surprised by how heavy he is. His little face is curled up in my breast, and I too start to sniff around at the bakery goods, wondering which dessert will please my Sabbath guests the most. An older woman leans into me imploringly. "Oy, a new baby," she says, her hand motions demanding that I produce my infant, who will be sniffed and nibbled at like the bobka. Babies simply command attention in Jewish communities, and like the bakery goods, adults often proclaim them "good enough to eat" and threaten to "take a bite." I, proud new mother and miles away from my own family, gently turn my handsome son to this woman's view. She visibly jumps back, and although she says not a word I can see her thoughts: a shvartzer—a black child. She scans my face, searching for Jewish features, then looks down at my son's wide nose and round eyes, and I can see her imagining my wild sexual escapades with a black man. She pulls herself together and smiles. She sees my little boy for the first time. "He's so sweet," she says. "Good for the two of you," and I somehow trust that she means this. She is not "really" racist, she would insist, just surprised. She went back to sniffing other bakery products; it is clear Aunt Sylvia wouldn't want us to bring home this sweet dessert.

The Jewish community, of course, is a tribe without borders. Jews are black and white, Chinese and East Indian, Arabian and Israeli. I have a book of international Jewry, and there are two pictures I love. One shows a Southeast Asian woman wearing a sari and a *bindi*, taking the chapati bread out of the big tandoori oven. The caption reads, "A Jewish woman preparing for the Sabbath." The other picture shows a Japanese man with a yarmulke and tallith standing in front of an opened Torah. The caption reads, simply, "A rabbi." In my son's room is a small picture mailed to me by a friend months before my son's adoption. It shows a congregation—men, women, and children—standing in front of their shul: All are American blacks.

Despite these images, racism is powerful, and American Jews are mostly the descendants of Eastern Europeans. In America it is our whiteness that has been our ticket, and who can resist what seem to be free tickets for a piece of the Apple Pie?

I decided not to circumcise my son. I did not think of this as a "heavy" decision. It is consistent for me with my values about bodies and sexuality and holistic health care. I was shocked by the intensity of others' reactions. My Jewish friends who never celebrate Shabbat or attend shul, who are tattooed and pierced, who are nonmonogamous radical dykes, insisted that circumcision is part of the holy covenant and that my son (read: "your black son") would never be accepted as a Jew if he had a foreskin. I struggled to find a local shul that would allow us a naming ceremony without circumcision. I wound up screaming at people on the phone for their ignorance, heterosexist assumptions, blatant white racism, and rigid Jewish orthodoxy. So I created and planned a beautiful ritual that followed the general guidelines of the Brith Milah and incorporated the less traditional rituals of a girl's naming ceremony. We also poured libations to the African gods; Shaiyah's Uncle Felix invoked the presence of the Yoruba deities Yanayah and Shango. I chanted the holy names of Ganesha, the elephant-faced god from India who protects children. Loved ones, including my son's biological cousins and his aunts—Jewish, African-American, and West Indian— surrounded us. We stood in a circle of protection, creating our families from the flesh of our bodies. My son is a Jew because he is being raised to be a Jew with all his flesh intact.

When I first decided to have a child I began the way most lesbians do: seeking donor semen and choosing between "known" versus "unknown" options. The process of choosing donor semen involves making endless choices, including hair and eye color and reading through piles of biographical profiles. Decisions about race also need to be made. One sperm bank color-codes their semen vials "white," "black," "yellow," and "red"; and someone from another bank told me that Jewish donors were in demand the most because people believe they are the smartest.

I considered inseminating with a Mexican donor. A Puerto Rican friend was appalled. "How will you sing lullabies to this child?" she asked. "You don't even speak Spanish." She thought it was racist of us to even consider this and ended the conversation. A white colleague, also a lesbian and who was also struggling with infertility, told me she was using a "Hispanic" (her word) donor. I asked her how she intended to address issues of the child's culture. She looked at me dismissively and said, "The child is American," and she too ended the conversation.

"Creating" biracial children brings up different issues from transracial adoption. One biracial friend said, "It's different if you love someone of a different race [as her parents did], but to purposely create children who will have to negotiate— that's just not fair." A black friend said, "You don't just create kids to 'match' the kid you have." Another black friend said, "I'm honored you would consider birthing a black child; it proves more to me, more than anything you've ever done, that you are truly not racist." And yet another friend says, "You must do this, or your son will be the only person of color in the family."

Living in a racist culture makes all decisions involving race suspect. Any choice made in picking a donor has racial and political implications, including choosing a white donor. Although it is often a less conscious decision, it is no less suspect.

❖ ❖ ❖

My friend Joel is a single Jewish gay man parenting a black son. Joel wakes up from the following dream: His son comes home from school speaking in a thick black dialect. He strains to understand him, but he cannot.

Before Joel became the parent of an African-American child he did not consider himself racist and did not think that the lives of white and black Americans were all that different. Now he knows that, as much as he loves his son, he may never understand certain things about him; he worries that they cannot speak the same language. He says, "There are certain things we don't know about ourselves until we cross that bridge." Jana Wolff, in the wonderful article "Black Unlike Me," on interracial parenting, says it is like waking up from "a deep, white sleep" (*The New York Times*, February 14, 1999). I have come to learn that many white people in my life were previously ignorant of their white skin privilege—not just asleep, but damn near in a coma. What Joel does not say is that when we cross that bridge, there is no turning back.

I pick up my infant son from day care and read his daily note, which says, "Today we learned how to make turkey sounds and Indian sounds." I am outraged and complain to the school. "Indians make the same sounds all people do. They talk," I tell them. "Indians are not animals that make sounds, they are people like you and me. It matters that even an infant is not taught that Indians make sounds like animals." I know I would have complained even if my son were white. I do not know if I would have pulled him out of the school, which I did immediately.

I do not think that being the white mom of an African-American child has made me more conscious of racism. I do not think it has made me a better antiracism activist. What it has done is point the rage of racists in my personal direction; it has made me more vulnerable.

Although white racists have now targeted me as their enemy, it doesn't mean I am any more welcomed into communities of color or able to assist my son in acculturating within black culture. Jana Wolff says, "It must be hard for a child to have as tour guides parents who are tourists themselves. The risk is that the culture being visited will be reduced to its souvenirs."

I call a black friend and ask her to help me braid my son's hair. She says, "Black people spend way too much time dealing with their hair. I was tortured as a kid. Don't do it to your son. Let his hair just be. Don't worry so much about it." I repeat this to another white adoptive mom. She says, "That's really bad advice. You're being held to different standards than she would be. Let her kids be wild; you keep your kid's head looking neat."

When my son gets chicken pox, I send an E-mail to a black friend: "What should I use to prevent his skin from scarring?" She says simply, "Cocoa butter and vitamin E." She does not lecture me about black skin. She does not tell me, "If you were black, you'd know the answer to that," which another friend says. She accepts that I am a tourist and gives me directions. When I get chicken pox four weeks later I discover that cocoa butter and vitamin E work really well on white skin too.

My partner and I have spent the last few years of our lives engaged in a long conversation about where we should live. Wherever we live we have to sacrifice something. If we live in a mixed-race neighborhood where our son will grow up comfortably seeing other dark-skinned people and nelly dads and butch moms, we give up our dream of living in nature and having our son free to spend his growing years knowing safety and connection to the earth. But if we live in the country, we commit to driving miles each week to maintain any kind of Jewish community or queer community or black community. Is this the price we pay for fresh air and unlocked doors?

Our neighbors are moving "uptown." An African-American family with two small children, they are moving to a white suburb with big lawns and safe streets in order to put their kids in "good" schools. Another family, an African-American lesbian couple with children, lives in a small town outside our city. They are the only children of color in their rural school. These families know their children cannot be better armed than with a good education. Their children will be educated in white schools but come home to black families. We recently decided to pull my son from his multicultural day care across the street from our house and place him in a Montessori school 20 minutes away. This school seems to offer an excellent education, though it stresses our budget to send him there. He will be one

I soon discover, but to urge the treatment on to success.
he baby's other mother, the one who'd carried him and
n birth, does the first shift under the tent. I then take my
e with the baby, swaddled and comfortable in my arms,
pray to hear the quiet, calm sounds of breathing instead
e labored and anxious high-pitched wheezing.

ere is nothing to do inside the tent except hold the baby
nope for the best. I realize that this is the first truly quiet
we have spent together since his midsummer birth. The
urs of labor, the agonizing decision to perform a C-sec-
and the baby's emergence from the open belly of his
mom were events of dizzying agony. He was born cov-
n his own bodily waste, then whisked off to the nursery
monitored for breathing problems. I was exhausted, wor-
nd also reeling from the reality that we would be rais-
son. With my emotions on the surface after a grueling
ntic day, my studied indifference to gender gave way to
of lesbian-feminist political reflexes. I was wrestling
y disappointment and anxiety that he was not a girl.
me point soon after, the baby stopped being a boy and
being our child. All those physical activities—feeding,
g, bathing, carrying, and rocking—they're all designed
ct you from any preexisting notions you may have had
into this experience, from the very romantic baby-love
the worst fears of parental incompetence. The experts
"bonding." During those first three months his other
d I established equal parenting roles, rotating the
routine and diaper changing. She did breast-feed the
t we soon found that he would also accept her milk
ttle. So I fed him too. I guess, then, during that time
were bonding. But it wasn't until the hour in the tent
ly adhered.

ick plastic makes the outside reality appear other-
lurry, and misshapen. The baby and I are awake,
t each other. All of my senses are heightened. I am

of the few children of color in his school. He will not come home to a black family.

Do we send him to an inner-city school, where he will be around more kids of color so he will never become a tourist among his own people? Or do we send him to the best schools we can, giving him a good education—which is the sharpest weapon we can give him to succeed in this racist society—while risking a sense of estrangement from other black people?

We make our home on the borders. Living Jewish lives, we are still outside the Jewish community because we are queers raising a black child. As out lesbians we are suspect as too radical because we are butch and femme, and too conservative because we are parents. As white parents raising a black child we have lost our membership to the white world but have not gained admission to the black community.

Arriving home from work, I open the door and smell chicken soup cooking on the stove. My son runs up to me, yelling, "Momma, you're home. Let's go light the candles." He smells of cocoa butter and macaroni, good enough to eat. On the table are the Chanukah menorah and the Kwanza kinara. My son wears his yarmulke, standing between his two moms who adore each other. He is growing into a tall Jewish black man, the son of proud butch and femme lesbian parents. It is done; we are home.

Glossary

bindi: (Sanskrit) red dot worn on the third eye to show devotion to God among East Indians

bobka: Eastern European sweet bread

Britt Milah: (Hebrew) ritual of the covenant of circumcision, performed for Jewish males at eight days of age

chapati: East Indian unleavened wheat bread

davenen: (Yiddish) to pray the prescribed prayers of the liturgy

Kwanza kinara: the candelabrum lit on the African-American holiday of Kwanza

shuckle: (Yiddish) to move back and forth rapidly in prayer
shul: (Yiddish) synagogue
shvartzer: (German, from *shvartz*) black, refers to African-Americans, used in a derogatory manner
tallith: (Yiddish) prayer shawl
tushies: (Yiddish *tokhes*) bottom, buttocks
yarmulke: (Yiddish) skullcap

I wish to thank Luz Marquez-Benbow, Joel Greenberg, Morgan Tharan, Kendra Lloyd, Sundance Lev, and Pam Michaels-Fallon for their thoughtful feedback. I am, of course, solely responsible for the content of this essay.

On Biology, Destiny, and Divorce
by Cindy T. Rizzo

November 1986

There is a separate emergency room Maimonides Hospital in Brooklyn. As series of large double-door entryways I that because it impresses me. We are because the baby, only three months ol ning a fever, but because as the sun se Maimonides Hospital is being over worth of the broken bones and w Orthodox Jews. Although health matte one to override the Sabbath comman ness, if not life-threatening, that wou tion is probably open to scholarly del the setting sun, hoping the baby wil

The staff actually accepts our ver the matter. Their diagnosis is bron placed in a tent where pure moist open his little breathing passages. him under the clear plastic cover

bal
T
give
plac
and
of t
T
and
time
12 h
tion,
other
ered
to be
ried,
ing a
and fr
years
with r
At s
started
changi
to distr
coming
stuff to
call thi
mom a
bedtime
baby, bu
from a h
he and
that I tr
The t
worldly,
looking

listening intently to his breathing, watching the movement of his chest, the color of his round face, ruminating on the small amount of light-brown hair on his head. He is wearing soft cotton overalls (red with little feet) and a white long-sleeve shirt. Even in his distress he is the essence of softness. The air is pumped into the tent silently. The only sound is the baby's breath heaving through his chest—that interminable wheezing.

"Breathe in the air, sweetheart," I whisper. "Let this help you. Let this help you."

It is more of a prayer than an admonition. He must get through this. So much lies ahead outside this tent, outside this hospital.

June 1994

Finalizing my second-parent adoption of the kids takes about ten minutes. We are in the judge's chambers in Norfolk County, Mass. He is tall, middle-aged, lawyerly, a nondescript judge out of central casting, complete with long black robe. He reads our petition, the stack of testimonials attesting to our home life, the children's schooling, our connection to Judaism. Who wouldn't be impressed? He sits in his black leather judge's chair and signs the papers. He offers the boys lollipops. We take pictures.

At last I am an official parent. I can sign things, I can make decisions, I can get custody. I should be happy. I should be relieved. And I guess it is assumed that I should be grateful. Instead I am annoyed. Annoyed that we had to pay a lawyer for this, that we had to take time off work for this, that we had to do it at all. I was their mother before this happened as much as I am their mother now. This formality changes nothing.

That day as we drive home from court, I do not think of all of the nonbiological lesbian mothers who live in states that don't recognize second-parent adoption. I do not think of all of non–bio moms whose former lovers have cut them off from their children. I do not know yet that in the near future I could have been one of those who got cut off or who was encouraged to slowly fade away in favor of the new partner, the new and improved non–bio mom. All I think about that day as we celebrate over a late-morning breakfast is how this adoption should have been official all along. It should have been included with the baby's birth certificate, a take-home item inserted into the hospital's tote bag, mixed in with the baby-care literature, the free diapers, and the blue-striped blanket.

But soon, too soon, my adoption papers will become a life raft, something I will cling to as my now ex-partner and I negotiate joint custody of our children. These rights will allow me to advocate for equal time, equal authority, equal input. They will enable me to establish my life with my children separate from their other mom and her new partner. In short, they will enable me to be empowered instead of beholden. I will look back on that day in the judge's chambers at the Norfolk County Probate Court, and at last I will be grateful.

1999

I guess I have always been a militant non–bio mom, unable to agree that it is either relevant or appropriate to focus on my status. In fact, I have suggested that it is downright offensive to do so. The context in which I live and parent my children supports that position. My sons were born into a community of coupled lesbian moms who, with only one exception, thumbed their noses at biological privilege. Some of us hyphenated our children's names. We all changed day care forms to read *mother* and *mother* instead of *mother* and *father*. We scrupulously shared all aspects of child rearing. Many of us had our children call us "Mommy" and "Mama," while some preferred their children to call them by their first names. The non–bio moms among us rejected the term "coparent" as an expression of inferiority. We were all just parents. Yes, there was a birth parent, but she was not to be thought of as the *real* parent.

Yet as time went on I began to draw a distinction between bowing to biology and ignoring it altogether. Children, as most who are raising them (or dealing with them a lot) know, will seize on anything an adult is actively trying to minimize. An effort to pooh-pooh the biological connection of a child and one mom will ultimately be faced with a countereffort by the child to obsessively focus on genetics. In my own situation, there is no getting away from the fact that my youngest son looks exactly like his biological mother and shares most of the same personality traits as she and her own mother. So I talk to the children about their seemingly inherited characteristics, which encompass everything from an ability to easily learn foreign languages to sneezing when first looking up at the sun. Just as they have inherited a cultural or ethnic heritage, my children to an extent have inherited a biological heritage. And I am a great believer in celebrating with them all aspects of what makes them who they are. In line with that thinking, however, I feel it is appropriate for me to take credit for a few things coming from my side of the family. My oldest son has a great appreciation for humor and a love of popular culture. He is also a budding writer. These are traits and talents that I would venture to say he has developed from and through me. So while I'm willing to give biology its due, I am unwilling to concede the entire inheritance issue to it.

These musings on biology and destiny would be pretty much complete had it not been for the divorce. The cause of the breakup—my unexpected and summary dismissal in favor of the "one true, great love"—has set up a difficult and competitive dynamic that has forced me to reexamine the whole *non–bio mom* label, particularly as I grapple with my feelings about the person who has been granted the title "stepmom."

Over the past few years two of my closest lesbian friends and I have created a little "divorce club," in which we strive to stay on the same every-other-weekend custody schedule with our kids so we can have dinner or go to the movies together on those off weekends. We talk about what all divorced parents talk about: our kids, our nonexistent love lives, and our exes. But I am the only one of us whose ex-partner has a new partner. So I am the only one dealing with the constant fear of being replaced. This fear is reinforced by the circumstances of my situation. My ex-partner and her girlfriend live in the same house where I once lived. They have all the advantages of a household headed by two adults (each can take a child to different activities, or one can go to a nighttime meeting, leaving the other one with the kids) while I struggle as a single parent. And, of course, there is all of my jealousy about the life they are building together as a couple.

The other big issue concerns the stepparenting role my ex-partner's new girlfriend has assumed with my children. Just to be clear, we are by no means in Snow White or Cinderella territory, so we're not talking "evil stepmother." No, if anything, this woman is the opposite. She works with children during the school year and spends her summers as a camp counselor. She is always ready to do creative woodworking projects or go hiking, skiing, or roller blading. Of course, this year-round child-involving activity maven is much more of a threat than the evil-stepmother type. In fact, she is so fabulous that a psychic once told me to chill out and let her develop a relationship with my kids. *Ahhhcchhh!* Is there no break for the jilted?

What all this leaves me with is a perpetual quandary about how much I am supposed to accept my children's having a second non–bio mom, *step* though she may be. Is it politically incorrect and hypocritical for me to want to deny her the same privileges and rights I fought so long to acquire and that I so passionately and desperately defend? Is she a thief who stole my family out from under me, or just the newest life choice my ex-lover made to become more fulfilled? Much as I try to disentangle them, my feelings about the divorce and the kids are still intertwined. What I tell myself—and anyone who'll listen—is that my recovery from this traumatic event, now three years old, is a process. I feel better about it today than I did a year ago, and I assume I will feel better still a year from today. I can't make myself do more than what I can right now. But since there's been an overall trend in the direction of progress from the worst of the devastation, rage, and depression I once experienced, I give myself a lot of permission to be exactly where I am at any given time. In the past few months, for example, my ex, her girlfriend, and I have been able to all go out to dinner with the kids, something I would have found unthinkable a year ago. But, by contrast, I have not yet been able to cross the threshold of the house that was once mine and is now theirs.

My second-parent adoption continues to be my insurance policy not only against the erosion of my parental status, but also against what so many other non–bio moms have done in the face of similar, though less legally favorable, circumstances: that is, simply giving up or serving as parent at the pleasure of the biological mom. I don't honestly know what my ex-partner would have done had I not been granted the second-parent adoption. My kindest supposition is that she would have tried to respect my parental role but that it would have diminished over time—in some part due to her acts and probably in part due to my own feelings of disempowerment. I am fortunate that I did not have to live in that alternate reality.

This morning I signed one of those consent forms that are required for children to go on class trips. After my signature I had to fill in "relationship." With a great sense of certainty and the force of the law behind me, I wrote in "mother." Not coparent, not nonbiological mom, and (with a degree of well-earned arrogance) not stepparent. Going all the way back to the agonizing yet peaceful time I spent with my son in the oxygen tent, through all the years that followed, I know that—with or without the judge's signature—mother is who I am. I see it in my little boy's face when he runs to greet me after being at his other house for five days. I see it in my now teenage son's actions when he quietly sits close enough to almost snuggle with me while we are on the couch watching TV. Truly those are the moments that define one's status. All the rest just ensure that what really is will continue.

Two Years and Counting:
Sperm Banks Prepare to Face the Test of Time
by Tzivia Gover

Many times over the years, Kathy, the mother of two sons, has been tempted to write a letter thanking the man who gave his sperm so she could raise a family. But as that fantasy comes one step closer to reality each year, she is increasingly hesitant.

Like hundreds of lesbians nationwide, Kathy and her female partner conceived their children using sperm from a bank that allows offspring to contact their donors when the children are grown. In 12 years Kathy's older son will be old enough to request from the sperm bank the information necessary to contact his donor dad.

"When I picture the possibility of meeting him, I feel a little embarrassed and wonder how he'll feel," says Kathy, who conceived her two children using the Sperm Bank of California. "I don't know if he knows that lesbians used his sperm, so it feels like it could be another coming-out process."

And while she and her partner have been up front with their boys, ages six and four, about their origins, there's no telling how they will process that information when they reach adulthood. "Will we need to go to therapy to deal with it, or will we be able to handle it on our own?" Kathy wonders.

Although Kathy still has some time to work through these questions, the day is just around the corner when the first meetings will take place between donors and offspring. In 2001 the first children who were conceived at the Sperm Bank of California using "willing-to-be-known" or "yes" donors will come of age. TSBC, located in Berkeley, was the first to offer women this option and was followed soon after by Pacific Reproductive Services in San Francisco and Pasadena. A few years ago, a third in California, Rainbow Flag Health Services, opened in Oakland, and has taken the concept of willing-to-be-known donors a step further.

These three banks, which supply sperm to women via clinics and physicians around the country, remain the primary sources for sperm from donors who agree up front to release their identities at some point. Other banks around the country say they'll help contact donors and query them about their willingness to meet their offspring, if they so desire, upon reaching adulthood.

Now, as the identity-release system comes of age, some are wondering if the banks will really be able to track the donors nearly two decades later. And when they do, what kinds of bonds will be formed between donor and offspring? Since most banks allow donors to provide sperm to between ten and 15 families, might these men suddenly be subject to a flurry of phone calls from their biological children?

Even as these questions remain unanswered, options for insemination with sperm from willing-to-be-known donors are proliferating, and these "yes" donors are becoming increasingly popular with lesbian mothers-to-be. At the Sperm Bank of California, where more than half of the clientele are lesbians, some 75% of inseminations are from donors who are willing to be known. But these days choosing a "yes" donor is only part of the identity-release process. At some banks, parents can buy a video of their donor, boyhood pictures, or essays that range from a few paragraphs to nearly 20 pages describing who he is, why he chose to donate sperm, and even what he hopes for his offspring. At Rainbow Flag a contract signed by both parties prior to insemination requires that parents and donors to meet when the conceived child reaches a year of age.

Meanwhile, the basic known-at-18 option has yet to be tested. In 2001 the first three children to have been conceived by "yes" donors will come of age and can request identifying information about their donors. In the following years the numbers will rise to ten, 20, and will finally level out to about 80 a year, according to Maura Riordan, executive director at the Sperm Bank of California.

"We're embarking on what I think of as a wonderful, progressive social experiment," says Susan Rubin, a medical ethicist on the board of directors at TSBC who says she is glad of the opportunity to create a system that will benefit all. But as with all pioneers, she is treading on unknown territory. "There are no precedents," she says.

So as the children who were born into this bold experiment celebrate their 16th birthdays, get their learner's permits, and plan for college, sperm bank personnel are scrambling to set up needs-assessment panels, draft legal agreements to be signed by donors and offspring, and set up protocols for the first donor-offspring meetings. Toward that end, the Sperm Bank of California has gathered a task force, which Rubin chairs, that includes donors, recipients, and a therapist who specializes in donor insemination issues, among others. Eventually panels of offspring will also be convened. Mothers whose children are now teens "feel excited but protective of their kids," Riordan says. Children who are now approaching adulthood are beginning to ask about half siblings and the possibility of meeting them, Riordan added. And although some older children are saying they don't want to meet their donors, most seem to want to make contact.

What that contact will consist of is unknown as yet. Most donors at TSBC, who signed a contract saying they would allow their vital statistics (full name, address, phone number, social security number, driver's license number, and date and place of birth) to be released to their grown offspring, say they envision a friendship, not a parenting relationship.

But despite all the preparations there is no way to predict results. "We're still in the learning process," Riordan says.

Many women, when inseminating with the sperm of willing-to-be-known donors, question whether the bank will be able to keep track of a donor's information for 18 years or more. What if the sperm bank closes? What if the donor moves and doesn't inform the bank? What if the donor changes his mind? He might have signed on to this project as a college student with no responsibilities of his own. When his donor offspring comes of age he might be married with a family and no longer want to be available to an 18-year-old he's never met.

In her position as director of All Our Families, Cheryl Deaner hears what's on women's minds as they embark on pregnancies through sperm banks. But most of their anxieties are focused on issues such as how many babies will be born to the same donor, what will happen if the donor wants to become too involved in their families, and so on. "The one I hear the least amount of complaining about is the known-at-18 system," she says. Most feel confident they are using a reputable sperm bank and that it will be able to follow through on its promise to provide information when the time comes.

Keeping records, though, may turn out to be the easiest part of the process.

Most banks back up their data, have checked their Y2K readiness, and have even planned for worst-case scenarios, such as a bank closing. TSBC has a private investigator to contact difficult-to-locate donors, a process that has already proven efficient when in emergency situations they've had to contact a donor for vital medical information. "The reality is, with some basic information, it's easy," Riordan says.

Rather than fretting over record keeping, ethicist Susan Rubin is thinking about promise keeping. Although the bald facts of what parents, offspring, and donor can expect are laid out in contracts signed before conception, hopes and expectations are less easily confined to terse legalistic sentences. "We're not promising a relationship. We're not promising a father or a friend. It's a very minimalist promise that we've made," Rubin says. Basically, the bank offers information. What the offspring choose to do with that information is up to them.

Liz Coolidge, who works with Fenway Community Health Center in Boston, where women can inseminate with "yes" donor sperm, says she wonders what form contact between donor and offspring will take and how the parties involved will react. "Men can go into this and donate sperm quite light-heartedly. They might be surprised when these kids show up or when a lot of feelings come up [regarding the reunion]."

And what about the adult child who is not the first—but the fifth or eighth—who comes knocking on a donor's door? How thin can a man, whose sperm may have been used to inseminate ten or even 15 women, spread himself?

While unanswered questions hover around these more open insemination procedures, it is clear from the experiences of children born through anonymous-donor inseminations in decades past that shrouding a donor's existence in secrecy does not always work. In fact, just as closed adoptions proved painfully inadequate to adult children who grew up with a passionate desire to know their genetic roots, adult children of donor insemination (born mostly to straight families) have also been voicing their discontent with anonymous-donor inseminations.

Donor insemination is nothing new and, in fact, dates back to the late 19th century. The practice gained popularity among heterosexual couples who were experiencing fertility problems in the 1940s, when fresh sperm was available in doctors' offices, usually from medical students.

In the late 1970s and early '80s lesbians began to investigate ways to start families together. Back in the early days of alternative insemination among lesbians, before we were having enough babies together to constitute a boom and before the risks of HIV infection were commonly understood, decisions about what role a donor would play in a family's life—whether he'd be a gay friend who would act as an uncle or whether he'd be the friend of a friend whose identity would never be revealed—was a matter of a few conversations and a handshake deal.

But an increasingly sophisticated understanding about the risks of HIV and other sexually transmitted diseases, along with the sheer numbers of lesbians who wanted to get pregnant, brought more and more women to sperm banks, clinics, or doctors who would inseminate them.

Sherron Mills was working at a lesbian health clinic when she realized there were a lot of lesbians wanting to get pregnant. She approached the director of the clinic about offering a donor insemination service. When she was turned down, she struck out on her own and in 1980 founded Pacific Reproductive Service. Soon after the bank started, women began asking Mills about the possibility of making arrangements so their children could find out about their genetic history when they were grown. Just a couple of years before, TSBC had begun a similar program, and Mills was quick to follow suit.

By then children conceived by early attempts at donor insemination by heterosexuals had come of age, and they were making known their discontent with anonymous donors. When these children were conceived, straight couples were almost universally advised by their doctors not to tell their children of the donor's role. This was meant in part to help infertile fathers avoid feeling emasculated. But as these off-spring learned their parents' secret, many demanded to know who the mystery donor was. Like people who had been adopted, they yearned to know more about their biological beginnings. And just as adoption practices began to change, lifting the veil of secrecy, so did the practices surrounding donor insemination.

Although originally intended for use by heterosexual cou-ples who couldn't conceive, donor insemination has become an integral part of the lesbian baby boom. And it is lesbians, who have much less stake in keeping their method of con-ception secret (we can't, after all, claim to have conceived children without help), who have pioneered more open forms of donor insemination.

Sperm banks nationwide consitute a multimillion-dollar industry. And although only a handful cater to lesbians (in some states it is still a crime for doctors to inseminate women who are not married), the number of lesbian-headed families using these services is on the rise. At least 2,000 babies have been born, mostly to lesbians, through Pacific Reproductive Services and the Sperm Bank of California, according to statistics kept by those banks. Sperm from these two sources is shipped to clinics and doctors around the country. "We can't keep up with the demand for willing-to-be-known donors," Mills says.

These days Mills is not only concerned with keeping up with new demand, but also thinking about meeting the needs of the families who will soon be ready to cash in on the prom-ise that their children will be able to meet their donors.

Questions that were raised 15 years ago about how the bank would keep track of donors for 18 years and how, when the time came, the parties involved would make contact are about to be answered.

Personnel at Pacific Reproductive Services, for example,

are drawing up legal documents for donors and adult off-spring to sign. These contracts will reiterate their rights and responsibilities to one another and remind offspring and donors that further contact should be made only if both parties agree, that they aren't entitled to one another's assets, that they won't contact each other's family without consensual permission, and so on. "The donor made a commitment to meet the children one time, not to have a relationship with them," Mills says.

But at Rainbow Sperm Bank, where information is given to recipients when their child is three months of age and where donor and offspring meet when the child is one year old, relationships are far more complex. Director Leland Traiman's one-man operation (he does work with a medical director, who is not on staff) collects sperm from donors—mostly gay men—who want to play an uncle-like role in their offspring's life. So far the bank has about 20 donors, and Traiman reports about 12 pregnancies to date, with the oldest child not yet in grade school.

Although many question Rainbow's policy of matching up donors and recipients when offspring are just a year old, Traiman says he is running the sperm bank's equivalent of an open adoption program. "Sperm bank kids are half adopted," he says. "Just like all adoptees, they have the right to know."

Rights, and who has them, however, is at the heart of several controversies surrounding the Rainbow Bank. Some fear custody battles could ensue when donors become involved in young children's lives. Mills, of Pacific Reproductive Services, says she has heard numerous complaints about Rainbow's policy of mandatory early meetings between donors and recipients. She prefers the known-at-18 option because it limits potential legal complications. Even though California law states that the donor has no legal right to offspring in physician-assisted inseminations, Mills fears that if donors meet these babies and young children, they might try to challenge the law.

Traiman shrugs off such suppositions. "Some women are paranoid about custody because lesbians have a long tradition of losing custody to former husbands. But these aren't former husbands. These guys are donors and they're queer too," he says.

So far the biggest disagreement Traiman has heard between one of his donors and recipients is whether one donor could be called Dad. Traiman sided with the recipient in this case, arguing that a donor is not a father, and in the end all parties agreed.

A larger controversy surrounding Traiman's bank is a contract he requires potential parents to sign promising not to circumcise sons conceived from the insemination. This type of restriction has some wondering how much a sperm bank should be able to interfere in a family's life and whether such policies tamper with parental rights.

But Traiman, who has helped inseminate Jewish women but who has no Jewish donors at present, says that the circumcision issue is about the rights of the babies. "One woman saw it as an intrusion on her rights as a parent, but our perspective is that human rights are absolute. Would we help someone with a history of child abuse have another child? The answer is no." Rainbow's policy would remain in effect for Jews, who consider circumcision a sign of a covenant with God. "Circumcision is child abuse. Period," Truman says.

Of course, Rainbow's known-at-three-months option, along with its other stipulations, account for just one option from which lesbian couples may choose. But Deaner, of All Our Families, fears that women who are anxious to become parents may get so caught up in attempts to conceive that they put aside or try to minimize concerns about a bank's policies. That seems like a real danger: With so few suppliers of sperm from willing-to-be-known donors, some parents might feel they don't really have a choice and might go along with policies they would otherwise write off as too invasive.

The known-at-three-months option is also complicated by the fact that women don't meet the donors before the pregnancy takes place, but after the child is born. What if this man turns out to be someone you'd rather not share a 20-block cab ride with, let alone your child's entire life? Sure, his healthy lifestyle, brown eyes, and curly hair were what you wanted in terms of a gene pool, but what if he now wants to chat on the phone every day, and you'd just as soon not hear from him again until your kid graduates from high school?

When I was deciding to have a child in the '80s the idea of secrecy surrounding the donor suited me fine. My partner would be our child's birth mother, and as the nonbiologically related one in the family I had donor envy from the start. Whoever he was—whether we would decide to choose him from a catalog offered by a sperm bank or whether we'd enlist the help of an anonymous friend of a friend who would not know our identities and vice versa—I feared that this man would have more of a claim on our baby than I would. As far as I was concerned, our child would have two parents, my partner and me—and that was that.

Now that my daughter is nearing 11, time and experience have complicated my vision of the donor's role in her life, and I am relieved that we chose a route that will allow us to help point her in the right direction should she one day want to find him.

Still, I can't help wonder at the plethora of options these days. If it is true that a donor is, as so many of us tell our children, just a nice man who donated his seed so we could start a family, would we really need to gather round the television set to watch him on video? Would I want my daughter to be cherishing an essay we purchased from a sperm bank in which the donor explains why he decided to donate his sperm? Or even what his favorite hobbies are? Although sperm bank personnel—and even most lesbian moms I've spoken with—say more information helps curb fantasies about a Donor Dad in Shining Armor, I wonder. This level of detail makes it seem that the donor is coming so far out of the shadows as to become a vivid personality—however absent.

Mills, of Pacific Reproductive Services, where lengthy biographies about donors and their biological families will soon be available to recipients, disagrees. "The definition of a parent is someone who raises a child, but the donor is just a donor. Someone who donated his genetic material," she says. "Our purpose was to let kids learn about their genetic history to satisfy their curiosity—not to have another parent."

Deaner agrees. Her son has a donor, not a father: "Taking it to the absurd, if you have a liver transplant, does that make the [liver donor] a part of your family?"

Even if he's not part of the family, the donor is a presence of sorts. And at some point he may have contact with the adult children and parents whom he helped make a family. At that time a new set of issues is raised in terms of how to incorporate him into the adult children's lives. What will it be like for an 18-year-old to actually be in contact with the man who was paid anywhere from a dollar to a couple of hundred to supply the vials of sperm that sparked her into being? Will the revelation of this mystery man be gratifying or horrifying?

As the time approaches for Deaner's family, she says she hopes her son will seek out his donor. "I hope he goes and meets him and they have a nice cup of coffee and a nice talk," she says. "I don't expect him to have a father-son-relationship. He has his own family." But she's in no rush. "I'm glad I have another eight years to wait," Deaner says.

Ride That Wave: Queer Parenting and AIDS
by Laurie Bell

For Caleb and Hannah

In 1999 I celebrated the tenth anniversary of my lesbian mothering. I take up these ten years as a very particular era not only out of a sense of grandiosity about my own parenting, but also because it is during this period—since the Berlin Wall came tumbling down and the face of progressive politics has been transformed worldwide—that we have witnessed the emergence of queer family as an increasingly evident aspect of our progressive political agenda and discourse.

AIDS, as San Francisco activist Eric Ciasullo maintains, is "the water we are all swimming in." During this decade and in these uncertain waters we have become a community intensely engaged in the births and the deaths that form the contours of the life process. How has confronting the demands of both AIDS and queer parenting simultaneously shaped our experience of each, since they have emerged in tandem with one other? What do we bring to our parenting from the curious mix of this burst of life and this burst of death in our lives?

I have certainly recognized in my leap toward parenthood the obvious intersection with the intense presence of AIDS. My parents met at a hayride; my son's parents met at an AIDS committee meeting. Before the excitement of a positive pregnancy test came the tears of relief for the negative HIV test result. Our first postpartum outing was to the hospice and into the outstretched arms of one who had vowed that he wasn't going anywhere until he had held that baby. And then, not long after, another outing to the memorial service in his honor. My child's first parade was from the vantage on top of the AIDS Committee float on Pride Day. But I also sense not only that our leap into parenthood was contextualized by the proximity and enormity of the AIDS epidemic in each of our lives, but also that our motivations in taking such a leap were deeply influenced by the experience of living within an epidemic, though we could not have understood ourselves in this way at the time. But it seems difficult now to deny the possibility that the resolve to get procreative, to begin a lifetime focused on birth and growth and development, was an instinctive response to the crisis of infection, illness, and death that surrounds us. As baby boomers are the population explosion that recalls the Holocaust of the Second World War, so too the queer baby boom testifies to the battle we wage with the AIDS epidemic.

During my child's first years the water we were swimming in was a tempest, with so many deaths and concerns swirling around us. There was so much to do so quickly. Prevention, education, lobbying, civil disobedience, hospitals, fund-raising, demonstrations, outreach, coalition organizing, care teams, and memorials—not to mention diaper changes, night feedings, child care, and chicken pox. Ten years later I look out at the ocean from the shore at Provincetown during Family Pride Week, and a sea of children, with their queer parents looking on, ride the waves on boogie boards and explore the depths with masks and snorkels. At night the bonfire that has at other times blazed on the beach holding vigil for those we mourn now serves to roast marshmallows for the children who delight in their sweetness and warmth.

My sense of joy becomes caught in the undertow of fear that raising children within our queer homes and communities puts us at risk of forgetting. Caught up in the beauty of these young lives, will we forget the lives that have passed? Will we avoid the grief that remains with us? Will we ignore the work that is still to be done?

I see two childhood friends, women now, who meet again in the midst of playful face painting, and I watch them draw close to share talk of the mutual childhood friend they loved and lost and the child born right afterward who is now an ongoing concern. Just as suddenly, I am reminded that raising children within our homes and communities is also filled with our remembering.

When I was young a childhood illness mostly kept me out of the water and watching from the sidelines. When AIDS came crashing onto our shores it seemed as if we were drowning or throwing lifelines as best we could. As I jump into the surf with my ten-year-old and we ride the waves together, I am awestruck to find I am at last learning to swim—or, at least, to feel some comfort in the water in which we are swimming.

Naïveté in Parenting:
An Excerpt From a Sept. 1999 Interview With Susie Bright

Ten years ago, when I made my first appearances at lesbian and gay centers, we were in basements with leaking pipes, talking about fist fucking and dental dams, discussing concrete sexual issues. Now the centers have beautiful, trendy improvements because of grant monies, and there are AA meetings on every floor. Now the only thing anyone wants to talk about is babies, babies, babies.

What strikes me during these conversations is that there has been a tremendous amount of naïveté in the lesbian parenting community. In the old days we asked each other really stupid questions like whether we were going to let our daughters wear dresses. We had no idea that there are an incredible number of other issues facing parents. You have to pick your battles: Either our kids brush their teeth, eat their vegetables, stop screaming, or are allowed to wear a dress. Feminism is a great start on most things, but there are so many issues that are not decided by how you stand on sexism. Where do you stand on discipline? What is your stand on money issues, on cleanliness? There's nothing that Gloria Steinem has said that is going to help us with those issues. We've been so worried about pink or blue clothing that we haven't been prepared for sleep deprivation or the loss of spontaneity in our personal lives, for example, because we were so caught up in our Right On, Sisterhood shit. There are too many other battles to take on the dress question.

And as lesbian parents we didn't know any of these things because we have always been so cut off from parenting. If you're straight and you're heading into a relationship and you think of having kids, there's this sense that you've been training for this all your life. Many straight couples do serious counseling on how they want to raise kids. Not everyone, of course: A lot just get knocked up and get married. But even in shotgun marriages there have been resources there for a couple for decades.

This has shown me that, regardless of united political philosophies, one's cultural background about child raising is overwhelmingly the biggest influence in the way one parents. The lesbian parents who were in the audience at the community centers, for example, had nothing in common as lesbians. What they had instead was an almost unshakable connection to their families of origin because as parents their values were related—either in rebellion or acceptance—to their upbringing. In heterosexual situations, for example, where people marry early and stay close to home, they have the advantages of similarity and compatibility, of life and of parenting, by virtue of their similar geographic origins.

Gay people, on the other hand, flock to urban centers where there's no common geographic background—the cities are polyglots of geographies. You can't take for granted that you think about money in the same way, eat the same way. And lesbians have no ritual for talking about raising kids. It's just so new for us.

So here we are, trying to figure this out, and in its most naive form you see couples who come from completely different backgrounds who fall in love and get swept up in the desire to have a baby. But they're not from the same place, and during the ten years since puberty they haven't been talking about how to raise kids. They don't know anything.

As a class of people, we have been so denied the joys and satisfaction of parenting that we have developed very romantic ideas of what it would be like. It's similar to people who have never had any money or never left the country. We don't know the reality of it. Like so many things in the lesbian utopia, the image is instantly shattered the minute the couple actually begins to parent.

Brave New Family
by Kimberly Mistysyn

Once upon a time, the only acceptable form of family consisted of one male breadwinner, one female housekeeper, and two or more children, with at least one of them being male. As the family format evolved to reflect our changing economy and society, this previous model became the "ideal" family. Increasing change has brought about a high rate of divorce and separation; the discovery of the dysfunctional dynamic in families that endeavor to mirror, on the surface, the ideal family; and the ever-growing liberation of gays, lesbians, bisexuals, transsexuals, and transgendered individuals has forever changed the definition of the ideal family structure. The number of parents or their gender can no longer define the ideal family. Love, support, understanding, trust, and communication are now the only acceptable defining characteristics for a family. Our laws are constantly changing to allow individuals without blood ties or the legal marriage link to consider themselves members of a family they created. This new millennium will see these brave new families continue to evolve and challenge society's rules and regulations.

Ours is one such brave new family, consisting of two gay moms, two gay dads, and our son. Let us tell you about our son's world.

Kyle was planned a year in advance. We chose not to go the expensive route of buying sperm and instead broached the idea of sperm donation with the dads, David and Clarke. The plan was pretty simple. I had already been charting my cycle and was taking folic acid. Clarke and David are an intergenerational couple; David, being the younger of the two, was our actual choice for "sperm donor cum laude." We wanted primary custody to our potential bundle of joy, and we hoped the dads would play an active role. As soon as the baby was born we wanted David to sign an affidavit giving up his legal rights to our child, thereby allowing Cynthia, the non–bio mom, to adopt our child. To cement the deal we all signed, with witnesses in tow, a nonlegal document outlining our mutual agreement to these terms and additional concerns should something happen to me during childbirth. We all went into this with our eyes wide open—love, trust, and communication being the crucial elements.

Babymaking was exciting, funny, nerve-racking, and, thankfully, quick. Cynthia sterilized the artichoke-heart jars by the dozen (actually eating their previous contents as well), the dads were at our beck and call with the fresh sperm, and the syringe was engaged with great pomp and ceremony. By the second month I had conceived. We told the dads of our success by giving them a gift-wrapped pregnancy predictor test with the confirmation displayed.

Our happiness knew no bounds as we prepared for a completely natural home birth with midwife and family members present. The dads attended all our visits with the midwife as well as our prenatal classes. And, as is usually the case with best laid plans, our son was born in a hospital—after an induction, an epidural, and an emergency C-section with only Cynthia and David allowed in the room. Kyle's due date had originally coincided with National Coming Out Day, but he decided that would be a bit too perfect and he aimed for our Canadian Thanksgiving weekend instead. He does, however, have a pink birthstone.

From the day Kyle was conceived to his present age of 21 months, life has never been dull. I do not mean to imply that just having a child makes life a roller-coaster ride, although it certainly has many similar moments. I mean to say that four parents and one child is enough to make one positively dizzy. When parents-to-be ask for advice, we laugh and say, "Every child needs four parents." The advantages might seem limitless. None of us needs to take several days off from work when Kyle is sick, because there are four of us to share the workload. Kyle has more love and attention than most children dream of. If one of us is sick, we can call on someone else to watch him as needed. Kyle loves his books, and he has already learned that each of his parents will read the same story in a slightly different way, so he will take the same book to each of us and listen eagerly each time. As Kyle has grown older the dads have taken him every other weekend for a two-night sleepover—we get a break, and the dads spend quality time with their son. We have been asked if that might be just as bad a situation as a child being shuffled between parents in a divorce situation, but Kyle does not experience any hostility or anger in our sharing time with him. He thoroughly enjoys his weekends with his dads and comes back happy to see his moms again. Clear communication is the only way our arrangement could work. In the long run, we really do feel like one big happy family, and it seems to flow smoothly. But we do pay a price for that: hard work.

I spent four days in the hospital, as is standard practice now after a C-section. When we finally went home with our new son the dads came by to visit every night. Our first challenge came two weeks after Kyle's birth, when I felt that if I had to breast-feed any longer I was going to have a nervous breakdown, and how could I be such a horrible mother for not giving the best possible food to my beloved son...to say that I reviled the feel of the baby sucking at my breast is no exaggeration, and I had not been at all prepared for that sensation. I had assumed I would love breast-feeding since it was so natural (just as I had thought I would glow when I was pregnant). So I found myself asking the dads for their permission to introduce the bottle. This was when we first realized that our relationship with the dads was now quite different. I should not have needed anyone's permission to stop breast-feeding, but since we were all now irrevocably linked by this child I had been afraid of upsetting the applecart. There is a certain underlying stress that comes from being a new mom and trying to ensure that four parents can collaborate together peacefully. There is a constant consultation process that happens before any decision can be made, because there are four opinions to consider.

Our adoption of Kyle could not go through until we obtained his birth certificate when he was three months old, and we were very aware that David could change his mind about signing over his rights to Cynthia. We wanted both dads to be blissfully happy with all our decisions, to ensure that the adoption process went according to plan. I should point out that this was not due to anything the dads said or did; it was simply the consequence of our situation. Ironically, it seemed as though the dads were also tiptoeing around us, being careful not to offend us because they wanted to ensure their visitation would continue. Of course, we knew they had nothing to worry about in that respect, and we even discussed all of these feelings, but there's no accounting for the way the mind works. Cynthia and I would not be able to relax until the adoption was finalized. Incidentally, the dads were wonderfully supportive about my need to introduce the bottle, and they actually benefited from it, as it allowed them to feed Kyle themselves, giving them more bonding time.

Both David and I, at separate appointments, had to sign affidavits allowing Cynthia to adopt Kyle. David did follow through and sign the affidavit, but he admits that it was much more difficult than he had expected. We still could not relax because there is a period of time allowed by the courts for David to change his mind. When we had our day in court and Kyle had his picture taken with the judge, it was the most wonderful feeling of relief! We hadn't been wrong to be so concerned because not many happy fathers will willingly do this for the non–bio mom, but we had picked our friend and donor wisely. David did go through with it because he trusted us enough to know that even without his legal rights we would grant him visitation with Kyle.

As Kyle grew, Cynthia and I invested in a house, and this meant we were no longer living quite so close to the dads. Communicating with the dads became a bit more difficult because suddenly we were consumed with our own separate lives, preparing to move and to fix up our new home. We also had to find a new day care center for Kyle. As always, we endeavored to ask for their opinions and input on the many choices we had before us. We moms had long talks about trying not to feel annoyed every time we had to ask the dads for their input, since we were Kyle's primary caregivers. The dads seemed to feel that we weren't consulting them enough or paying attention to their advice. The tension that resulted, and the sense that we were doing the best we could, prompted me to say that I was feeling some conflict and wanted to have a meeting about it. The last thing you want when you share the responsibility of a child is to be at odds for any reason. We were suddenly struck by the fact that we were even *having* a meeting to discuss conflicts. Pre-Kyle, we would get together and watch a movie or have an afternoon visit to enjoy a friendly, relaxed chat. Post-Kyle, we were all parents with no fun time to spare for each other because we were in touch enough with our daily parenting communications. We all seemed to share a relationship that was much closer than friendship, and yet, ironically, we were further apart. We discussed boundaries at our meeting. We moms pointed out that we had always understood that we would have primary decision-making privileges, but we would include the dads when we thought it necessary or appropriate. We felt that part of this setup included trusting us to make those decisions. By the time we met to have this discussion the dads had already concluded that it was not possible to expect us to confer with them on each item that popped up, since there are certain decisions that have to be made on the spot or by the parents who have to live with the consequences.

There are, however, specific issues that arise that must be addressed by all four of us. Although the dads did not seem to feel this was a huge issue, before the birth of Kyle we all had to agree on a first name for our child. We were lucky that the dads seemed content to go along with whatever we chose and, for our part, we tried hard to ensure that we passed on a part of David's name to his son, since Kyle was given my surname. I decreed early on that the child would get my surname, since I was housing him for nine grueling months. No one argued with me. Cynthia has an Irish branch in her family, so I wanted the child's first name to be of Irish descent to give a part of her family to him—hence, the first name Kyle. Kyle's middle name is the Hawaiianized form of David, to reflect my more unique family background and to give him his father's name. It was an unfortunate happenstance that Clarke was left out of the names we chose for Kyle, but we were probably considering the fact that Kyle is a first child for three of us, while Clarke has participated in choosing names for four children of his own.

The naming issue was followed by the circumcision debate. None of us are Jewish, so it was primarily a health concern. The dads did not know much about it, although one of them was circumcised. Cynthia and I knew even less and decided that it might be a good show of our faith in them to let this decision fall under their jurisdiction. In Canada circumcision is no longer automatically performed, and there is a fee to have it done in the hospital. As my pregnancy progressed and Cynthia and I discussed the topic with others, we decided we were against the concept of circumcision as a necessity and even regarded it as barbaric. Cynthia, who is not normally the emotional one of the two of us, became so disturbed that the dads might want our unborn child circumcised that she was even moved to tears. We felt we couldn't take the decision away from the dads, but we really couldn't ignore our feelings. In the end we compromised and decided that in keeping with our new four-parenting relationship, we had to tell them how we felt. Having told them, we would continue to let them make the ultimate decision, but if they still decided they wanted our child snipped, they would have to pay for it and make the arrangements because we would not actively participate. Eventually, before we knew we were going to have a son, the dads said that, after reading up on it and discussing it, they would not have the procedure performed unless our child made an informed decision about it later in life. We would have stood by their decision if they had felt strongly enough, but it made us feel all the more impressed that they took the time to do the research and that they made a responsible decision. I like to believe they appreciated our faith in them.

I am not a particularly religious individual. I am spiritual in that I believe in a god of some kind all around us, inside us. In this way I am more religious than Cynthia and Clarke. David was raised Catholic but has since abandoned his attachment to the church. When I announced that I wanted to christen Kyle they responded with surprise. The dads were curious as to why I would want to do this, and we discussed it at great length. Ultimately, they were fine with my vision of the christening, but if we had all come from different belief systems, yet another challenge would have been added to our complicated lives. When he was born I felt blessed that Kyle was a reality, and I wanted to give thanks in a spiritual way. I also wanted Kyle to wear the christening gown that had been handed down in our family for generations. We all agreed on a custom-designed ceremony at the dads' apartment, blessed by a priest friend of ours who had been ousted from the church for being a practicing homosexual. It was both intimate and gay. We moms selected the godmoms (Kyle has two), and we let the dads pick goddads (they chose one).

The dads are free of all obligations, including financial concerns. If they choose to take a trip out of the country for a month, they have no trouble doing so. We feel that the dads have the best of both worlds—parenting without obligations. In their defense, they have never said they would not contribute financially. They take Kyle for his haircuts regularly and pay for some of the items they need to keep in their home for him. We moms decided we should pay for Kyle's day care and other expenses that arise from having a child. It seemed only right, since Cynthia had legally adopted him. This also ensures that we have ultimate decision-making power. Not an easy task for two women with full-time jobs, and who have day care and a house to pay for. This decision also defines the number of children we can afford to have. To have another child, we would have to be free of some of our debts or allow the guys to contribute to some of the finances, which opens the doors to other issues. How we all relate to having Kyle will be an excellent indication of whether we could make it work with a second child. Theoretically, if the dads are happy with the way we are bringing up Kyle and can see that we make a great effort to include them, then their financial contributions with a second child shouldn't need to change things.

It takes the extra effort to keep things at an even keel. When Kyle gets letters from day care, we make sure he has a copy for us to pass on to the dads. On Mother's Day and Father's

Day the day care center is very good about sending Kyle home with a gift for both moms and both dads. When Kyle had his first accident at day care—a split tongue—we received the anxious call from his caregiver, who asked us to meet her at the hospital. On the way over I knew I should call the dads, but everything was happening too fast. Once I arrived at the hospital and knew Kyle was OK, I immediately placed the call. Arriving at the hospital had been an interesting experience in itself. Cynthia had arrived before me, and when I raced in and announced that I was Kyle's mother, I was informed that Kyle's mother was already there. This gave me a quick glimpse of the circus I could anticipate if, God forbid, anything serious ever happened to Kyle and all four parents were present. Luckily, I did not have to launch into an explanation of Kyle's life story, since the nurse rolled her eyes and told me to follow her. She obviously did not feel the need to question me further.

Kyle is just at that age where he loves to say a "night-night" and a "love ya" to us. We get many hugs and kisses from him. We do hope that he will always be as loving as he is now, but then there are those dreaded teenage years. There will also be the testing period, which may last longer than usual, with four of us to pit against each other. If Kyle is being punished with no television privileges, he may try to convince his dads to bend the rules, especially if his moms have forgotten to mention it to them. We trust the guys to check with us first if they suspect a ploy, just as we will have to be very clear in our communication with them. We also have to trust that the dads will honor certain rules we have established with Kyle when they have him for a weekend.

When Kyle was a baby David asked us a million methodology questions, such as if we fed Kyle on demand or only at specific times. David found that each of us had a different opinion, as did other mothers. We tried explaining that there was no right or wrong way, but what concerned us the most was the routine. We wanted to know that whichever way we decided best to approach it, they would continue with it so that when Kyle returned to us he wouldn't be confused by a sudden change. We wanted a certain consistency, and since we had Kyle 24 hours almost every day we felt this was in our decision-making domain. We also have a slight fear that as Kyle gets older he might prefer visiting his dads because he'll think of them as the "fun" parents.

Four parents might provide enough love to keep Kyle from becoming a sullen, angry teen. Or they might offer too much parental guidance for any one child to handle. When he starts to ask questions, we will proudly tell him how long we planned for him and how loved he is and how we worked hard to create him. As he grows there will be inevitable questions from schoolmates and explanations to teachers and principals, and we would all be fools if we did not prepare for the homophobia that will touch us and Kyle at some point, even in this more enlightened age. Some children are able to keep their parents' sexuality under wraps, but four parents are difficult to hide—especially when they all want to attend meetings with teachers and watch him participate in sports or concerts. We can only hope he will be so aware of the love surrounding him that he will be confident enough to stand up for what he has been brought up to believe.

Because this family consists of four adults with different desires and needs, conflicts do arise. Clarke is currently struggling with cancer and the ensuing chemotherapy. We moms want to accommodate his needs, and sometimes that means being flexible about having Kyle more often when we would usually have enjoyed a break. Clarke is also the one who doesn't have a biological or legal link to Kyle. Clarke has to be secure in that he is Kyle's dad because we say so and because Kyle recognizes him as such. Being the oldest, however, Clarke has the most life experience. He has been married, and has four grown children and many grandchildren. Clarke once said that being a father to his partner's son is a whole new role to him, and allows him the chance to do some things differently this time around. That brings me to David, who was over the moon the day Kyle was born. As I got to know David and saw that he was committed to being with Clarke, I knew he would be great father material. Our only concern with David has been his smoking. When we spoke about creating a child, he said he would start cutting back on his smoking and hoped to have quit by Kyle's birth. His heart was in the right place, but that didn't quite happen. The wonderful thing was that we could talk about it, although I will admit that I felt like a nag every time I asked. David has been fantastic about not smoking around Kyle and has cut down to an occasional cigarette. We continue to hope that David will be able to successfully quit and are happy that he respects our wishes around Kyle.

We moms are about to leave for a vacation without our son for the first time since his birth. This is a luxury most parents do not enjoy. But as we prepare to leave Kyle with the dads, we do feel some anxiety. We know the dads will take excellent care of him, but we worry about how much Kyle may miss us since we've never been away from him for an entire week. We also know Kyle is usually on his best behavior when he's with his dads because he does not get as much time with them, so he may not miss us much at all. This brings me to the sensitive subject of personal feelings, which does not usually get discussed. Parents experience a wide range of emotions when they coparent a child, and I believe this is especially true of coparenting with four parents.

Throughout my pregnancy I received heaps of attention from Cynthia, Clarke, and David. I had morning sickness at all times of the day in my first trimester, migraines in my second, and in my last trimester I battled gestational diabetes. Everything suddenly became very medical, but I was showered with support and love because I was sacrificing to have our healthy child. It was both horrible and wonderful at the same time. My pregnancy culminated in a huge baby shower that the dads threw for me as well, as the patience they afforded me when I was going through inductions and painful labor. The minute Kyle was born, attention shifted to our tiny miracle. The dads still had huge respect for the role I played in making this all possible and they have always told both Cynthia and me how much they love us, but I could feel the limelight moving from my now deflated stomach to our new baby. I know this is a common perception for many new mothers, but most new mothers probably weren't losing the attention of three key people at the same time, and I found the adjustment difficult.

Cynthia and I also went through a stage in which we felt competitive with the dads. Clarke and David lead busy lives, and although we never went out much before Kyle's birth, the sensation of being stuck at home by necessity after his birth frustrated us. If the dads came for a visit and talked about how tired they were from something or other they had been doing, we always tried to respond sympathetically, and then we found ourselves reminding them why *we* were so tired lately. My personal feeling was that they had the choice to be so busy or get some sleep, but we had no choice in the matter— our son's feeding schedule now ruled our lives. Our irritability about our lack of sleep made us envy the dads. And we saw some green over their ability to visit whenever they wanted while Cynthia and I had to parent full-time. The stress of early parenting caused many arguments between Cynthia and me, and we missed our carefree days, which we felt the dads were still enjoying. I also recall occasions when we were all together and someone would comment on how wonderfully behaved Kyle was. Whenever the dads would agree that he was a perfect angel I would immediately state for the record that Kyle had his not-so-great moments, to which the dads were not usually privy since they only see Kyle two weekends a month. I'm certain that the dads felt I did not always need to remind people of this. For their part, I'm sure they appreciate their freedom, but they probably wish they did not have to check with us every time they want to see Kyle, and probably would rather see him more often if it were not for their full-time jobs and the distance between our residences. Cynthia and I must remind ourselves that this is the price we pay for having primary custody.

Part of me will enjoy leaving Kyle with his dads for a full week to let them have a small taste of what our world is like, and yet I know I'm not being fair because Clarke is ill and has already been down this road with his own children. I think this time Cynthia and I will really feel sympathy for them if they tell us they are exhausted when our trip is over. The very fact that we are taking this trip was an issue of disappointment for the dads. Before Kyle was born all four of us would travel together sometimes, and we pledged that someday after we had a child we would all go on a holiday together. Although we would still love to do that and we thoroughly enjoy spending time with them, we moms are so desperate for time alone that we eventually had to plead our case. We invited the dads to join us, but specified that if they did join us, they would have to pay for Kyle because we couldn't afford it now and that Kyle would have to stay with them at night to give us some feeling of actual vacation. As it turned out, Clarke was not well enough to consider going, but we sense that they also feel that sharing a child has brought us closer together and yet further apart. We hope that as Kyle gets older and becomes his own person, it might be much more enjoyable to all travel together.

Since Cynthia and I have Kyle most of the time, we are usually more aware of Kyle's eating, sleeping, and behavior patterns. We tell the dads when Kyle is eating new foods or switching from whole milk to 2%. If Kyle has been taking a book to bed with him at night or a special stuffed animal, we tell the dads that too. From day one of my pregnancy the dads asked what equipment they would need to keep at their house for Kyle. At that point it was too early to know how our arrangement would finally evolve or in what pattern they would be having visits or overnights with Kyle. We knew they would need at least a crib, a stroller, and a high chair. Items such as clothing and bottles could be packed in a knapsack for visits with the dads. The dads, however, lead such event-filled lives that it took them a while to get these items. For example, they were waiting on a loaner crib from Clarke's grandson, who was about to outgrow his. In the meantime they borrowed our playpen for Kyle to sleep in, which was fine if they were willing to carry it each time.

Cynthia and I found ourselves trying to make it easier on them in any way possible. When Kyle was at the stage at which he was sitting and eating and the dads still did not have a high chair, we handed one down to them. If we received two of the same gift for Kyle, we would pass along the second one to the dads. When Kyle started brushing his teeth, we found it easier to buy two brushes and pass one along to the dads to make sure they would have it immediately. When Kyle started to show an interest in the potty, we passed on a potty so he could have one at both homes. This will come up again, as it will not be long before Kyle is ready to move into a bed; once he figures out how to get out of his crib, it will be dangerous to keep him in one. Since a bed is a large item, we have given Clarke and David plenty of advance warning that they'll need to begin preparing a proper room with a bed for Kyle. But, although we have meant well, Cynthia and I have to stop behaving as though we have to do everything possible to make things easy on the dads, since they have no such expectations.

Our biggest complaint about four busy people parenting is the scheduling headaches, especially when I was pregnant. I tend to be a very accommodating person (luckily, so are the dads), and trying to pick appointment times for ultrasounds and sessions with the midwife to include all four of us was a nightmare. We were thrilled to have the dads there, but I could never just call up and book an appointment for myself. And that is what life will continue to be like. For every appointment with a teacher, every concert, every vacation, every birthday party, and every Christmas, we will continue to confer over schedules with the dads. Not to mention all the extended family that comes along with having four parents.

Having discussed and anticipated these four-parent challenges, we moms would do it again in a heartbeat—we would do it again with Clarke and David, that is. We are all focused on Kyle, and that seems to make the hard work worth it. There is a special love among the parents that comes out of an arrangement such as this that continues to grow as our communication becomes easier and smoother. It enriches our lives and leaves us looking forward to the challenging future.

From Hostile to Helpful:
Parallel Parenting After a Mixed-Orientation
Couple Divorce
Amity Pierce Buxton, Ph.D.

"Welcome!" our Straight Spouse Network Web page says, its Anasazi hands reaching out to heterosexual spouses whose partners have disclosed being gay, lesbian, bisexual, or transgender. You may wonder what connection this international network has with queer parents. Well, the goal of the SSN is to help straight spouses to constructively get through the anger, grief, and pain of their spouse's coming out and to assist them in building bridges of understanding with their gay, lesbian, bisexual, or transgender spouses so that those who are parents can help each other develop parallel parenting plans in the best interest of their children. Reaching out, healing, and bridge building form our mission statement.

Since most couples break up after a spouse comes out, our concern is that the couple's relationship is not destroyed along with the marriage, especially if they have children. Children need both parents in their lives. Outside of abuse, neglect, or risk to a child's safety, little justifies the cutting of the child-parent bond, even if the parents break up. The children need both parents, and parents are either effective or ineffective as parents, regardless of sexual orientation or gender. We believe that hostile divorced parents can become helpful coparents if both of them find support to work through the postdisclosure upheaval in a positive direction. We not only believe it, but have seen it happen.

The network's cornerstone was laid in 1985 after my husband of 25 years came out. The Gay Fathers of San Francisco, noting my understanding of why he had remained closeted and how he had suffered in trying to do the "right thing," asked me to write a book on straight-spouse issues. They wanted to understand why their wives were angry—some so enraged that it was hard for the fathers to see their children often or at all. As I began to interview spouses across the country I discovered why the book was needed and how mutual understanding between spouses is critical for effective parenting. The straight spouse, in particular, is often key to the health and happiness of postdivorce families. One of my first interviews made that point. Frank, a gay father, told his story from his bed in the hospice where he was dying from AIDS. His former wife, believing the disease fit punishment for his being gay, was preventing their two children from visiting him. I observed that he and his children clearly needed to be together at that moment.

My book, *The Other Side of the Closet: The Coming-Out Crisis for Straight Spouses*, reports common issues spouses face and the many ways of resolving them constructively, information I hoped might help decrease the occurrence of such family tragedies. Yet, "a support group between book covers" was not enough. Providence drew me to the additional ingredient that was needed. Another interviewee, Jane Vennard, who headed a task force for straight spouses for what was then Parents and Friends of Lesbians and Gays

(PFLAG), asked me to be their contact for the mid Pacific region. In 1991, the year *The Other Side of the Closet* was published, she asked me to take over the task force. Soon it was renamed the Straight Spouse Support Network (SSN). Today SSN has spouse contacts in nearly every state and six foreign countries and roughly 40 support groups here and abroad, plus online message boards, telegroups, several Internet mailing lists, and a newsletter.

How does the network help mixed-orientation parents after disclosure? Why do its staff members continue their volunteer efforts even as requests for help mount daily? The more I talk with spouses and children, now totaling about 3,500, the more obvious the answers to both questions become. Coming out in a marriage is not just an individual experience—it's a family matter. Everyone is involved: mother, father, and children.

Disclosure within in a family occurs in waves, impacting each member in succession. First, the gay, lesbian, bisexual, or transgender spouse struggles to come to terms with his or her sexual orientation or gender. Next, when he or she discloses to the husband or wife, the heterosexual spouse faces the new information and begins to deal with it in some fashion. Finally, when their child or children find out or are told, they start the process of handling the new orientation or identity of their parent. Each family member deals with similar issues of sexuality, identity, integrity, and belief system but at different stages and from the various perspectives of spouse, gender, age, parent, or child. In addition, the children cope with their developmental stages of simply growing up. Thus, the household environment becomes somewhat turbulent. At any time anyone's emotions may erupt or be withheld only later to emerge, sabotaging attempts at honest discussion or negotiation.

During the first year or two after the disclosure, the euphoria of liberation for one spouse and the shock and disorientation of the other create an instability that does not lend itself to rational decision making or typical conduct on the part of either spouse. In this initial tumult, parenting responsibilities may temporarily leave the radar screen and children's voices go unheard, even by previously devoted mothers and fathers, straight or gay. If the spouses separate within these early years, as seems to happen more often for couples with a lesbian and a heterosexual man than for couples with a gay or bisexual man and a straight woman, the job of parenting becomes one of parallel parenting in two different homes, posing even more sources of dispute.

This period of discord after a spouse comes out is sometimes marked by sweeping generalizations, and based on false assumptions and stereotypes as well as pragmatic reactions to the disclosure. The straight wife's verbal expressions of anger may be seen as a sign of homophobia rather than an expression of hurt and pain from the disclosure. The lesbian wife may be viewed as anti-male rather than simply being more attracted sexually to females, or to a particular lover, or feeling more fulfilled with a lesbian identity. The straight husband's hostility may be seen as a personal attack, not as a way to deal with frustration at having his wife come out and leave in a short period. The gay husband may be perceived as a liar or a jerk rather than someone who struggled with fears of rejection because of homophobia and is now dealing with sexual needs that he never had a chance to explore. Working through these stereotypes to see the reality of the situation and to develop strategies to discern the wishes and needs of each spouse is possible. Getting to this point is more likely if both spouses have peer support and role models, and let enough time pass to bring about some measure of healing and distance.

For the heterosexual spouse SSN provides peer support and models of spouses who have capitalized on time's passage to work through disclosure issues. Recently, on one of our mailing lists, spouses who had been through the turmoil helped cool down the anger and encourage the rational thinking of a husband who was threatening a myriad of ways to get back at his lesbian wife who, after soulful deliberations, had decided to leave. As network director I shared those efforts with his wife so she would not think the whole straight-spouse world was conspiring against her and thereby might become less fearful for her children's welfare.

Based on my 13 years of working with spouses in this way and studying disclosure issues, the attitude of the straight spouse toward the disclosure and his or her partner plays a key role in how postdisclosure turmoil affects children. Straight parents become models for their children's perception and acceptance of the coming-out parent's new identity. However, freshly facing the new information about their partner's orientation or transgender status and feeling their spousal relationship threatened, heterosexual spouses find it hard just trying to understand the situation. That process takes time. In addition, straight spouses usually find themselves alone as they cope with their concerns. They too feel stigmatized by antigay attitudes or negative views of transgender persons. When they dare to tell others about the disclosure, the outsiders often minimize the issues, express anger, or encourage divorce. Many straight friends and family members see coming-out difficulties or a consequent divorce as a typical marriage problem, and some gay or lesbian friends cannot understand why the partner's disclosure is not celebrated and why the spouse cannot let him or her go gracefully.

Issues faced by straight spouses are unique, and the social isolation in which they find, or put, themselves magnifies the issues. Their most singular concerns center on their sexual rejection as a man or a woman; the challenge to their marriage; how having a "different" parent affects their children; perceived deception or betrayal by their partner; and a crisis of identity and belief system. Many tell themselves, *I wasn't man enough to keep her from becoming lesbian* or *I must be sexually inadequate if he turned to a man for sex.* Questions abound. *If my husband is really a woman, does this make me lesbian? Will I get AIDS? Can I trust anyone again? Will the children be teased? Will they follow in their mother's or father's footsteps? What about everything I was taught about homosexuality or transgender persons in my family of origin, school, church, or temple? What if people at our jobs find out...or at the club or the kids' school or the temple or church?*

The profound complexity of these issues makes it imperative that time be taken to resolve them. Generally, it takes two to three years or more to move from initial trauma to some level of transformation. The stages of this process, listed below, progress from meeting survival needs to reintegrating the broken pieces of their lives:

- shock, disorientation, denial;
- gradual facing of the pain and the reality of the disclosure;
- anger (which can turn to vengeful bitterness if untreated);
- acceptance of the situation and letting go of the past;
- grief (which can turn into despair if untreated);
- healing of body, mind, and spirit; and
- rebuilding identity, values, and belief system.

Given the long process of the spouse's journey from trauma to transformation within a volatile family environment, how does the SSN help spouses manage the roller coaster of emotions and day-to-day disasters? How do we help them resolve the complex problems, especially those that cause eruptions of anger leading to hostility between the two parents? By providing access to peers—others who have walked in their shoes along this path. Peers are the main resource enabling spouses to get through all stages in one piece, not letting anger linger as bitter vengeance or grief disintegrate into despair. Therapy, of course, also helps spouses handle personal or relationship issues, but many therapists have not yet had clients with this problem and are not equipped to help spouses resolve issues unique to a disclosure.

The SSN network of peers across the county and abroad offers personal support and resource information so that spouses no longer see themselves as victims, but as victors in their own lives—that is, authentic individuals who can move on in their lives without resentment and despair. Concurrently, we help them try to understand the other side of the closet so that they can preserve their children's bond with the gay, lesbian, bisexual, or transgender parent, and work on an equal level with their spouses or former spouses to create parenting plans that provide nurturing, safe, secure, and loving homes for the children.

To tap into this network, spouses often hear about us in the media, find us on the Web, read about us in a book such as this, or contact the SSN by mail, E-mail, letter, or telephone. Besides recommending books, we refer spouses to individual spouses or support groups (face-to-face, cyber groups on the Internet or AOL, or a telegroup). The goals of this peer interaction are to validate where the spouses are in their journey and to help them deal constructively with their particular circumstances.

Calling the SSN office may be a spouse's first contact with a peer. Surprised that they are not alone, many spouses let loose their whole story. Others simply ask for the nearest spouse or support group to meet their pressing needs. When a conversation moves into problem areas, the dialogue may sound something like this:

Spouse: He stayed out until 3 this morning without calling. When I told him I was angry about that he told me I was homophobic.
SSN: Well, that's not uncommon. It's hard to take someone's anger without becoming defensive. Have you tried using

"I" statements, such as "When you do this, I get angry?"

Spouse: Yes, but it doesn't work. He just keeps blaming me.

SSN: Sometimes to be heard one has to say things over and over and in different ways. But it's important to communicate your hurt and anger so that it doesn't get bottled up. It also helps husbands to know what you're angry about. It's not about his being gay in this case, but being late. Yes?

Spouse: Yes.

SSN: Just remember, you're not alone. Many spouses are in the same situation. You might want to read _____. And we have a couple of other wives struggling with similar issues. Would you like their numbers? There's also a support group nearby, if that might be of interest.

Spouse: Thanks, I'd like that.

The next peer with whom a spouse might interact is a state or country contact: a husband or wife who has gone through the coming-out crisis and gained perspective on the many ways of handling it. One former husband described his route to becoming a contact in a recent issue of _News & Notes_, the SSN newsletter: "When my wife told me that she was lesbian, well, I broke down. Mind, heart, soul—all shattered. That was four years ago. A year later I became a telephone contact for the SSN, and my acceptance was automatic, if somewhat hesitant. I hurt inside but knew that others hurt too, and I felt that we could help each other." Among the contacts is an Hispanic wife who is there for all Spanish-speaking spouses who contact us, especially those from Latin America.

Calls to contacts sometimes last an hour or more as the spouses share their pain and confusion with someone for the first time. As they talk, many find answers to their own questions or discover insights. The contacts then put callers in touch with other spouses in the region so they will have peers with whom to talk or upon whom they can call as "emergency therapists." Contacts also follow up by mailing articles on disclosure issues, the network brochure with recommended readings, and the SSN newsletter.

In addition to individual contacts, peer support groups allow wives and husbands at different stages of dealing with each issue to help one another on an ongoing basis. One wife from my group five years ago just called from her new home in Las Vegas. Having read an article in the *Las Vegas Review-Journal* about a local SSN group being formed, she wanted to offer her help to the new leader by providing newcomers a model of someone who had experienced the crisis they were now facing and who now, wiser and stronger, was in a new place in her life.

Special groups include subscription Internet lists and online message boards. Here spouses post as often or as seldom as they like, forming virtual communities of newcomers and veterans of the disclosure crisis. Individual messages are responded to, questions answered, concerns heard, and requests met by diverse spouses who range in age from 20 to 70, living in all parts of the country and abroad. (Sadly, these represent only those who have access to computers and are predominantly white and middle-class with some college education.)

Telegroups are the newest form of support, developed as a master's degree project by a spouse's relative in conjunction with a community service organization. Via conference calls spouses or couples talk with one another for an hour once a week for six weeks. These groups operate periodically throughout the year.

Through such peer interactions spouses gradually work through their unique issues to become self-confident and forward-looking. This means they can tune once more into their children's needs and take up the parenting task with their present or former spouses. Focusing on their parental roles, both spouses can join in a partnership that will assure their children that they are still loved by both their mother and father and, if a divorce has occurred, that they will be safe in either parent's home from any feelings or remarks that denigrate the other parent.

As for the future of SSN, reaching out to more spouses—especially those of color, those in the hinterland, and those without computers—is a major objective. We would like to expand links with other organizations that address marital issues, such as family service organizations, as well as therapists, clergy, and lawyers. We would also like SSN to be listed as a resource for coparenting classes, which are often court-ordered for couples filing for divorce.

Most of all, we would like to institutionalize SSN so that support will always be available to any spouse in any community at any time. The heterosexual spouses need help in rebuilding shattered lives no less than the spouses who come out—our children's future is at stake. They want and need safe, secure, and loving homes. To help create such homes, straight spouses need peer support to work through their anger and grief so they can rejoin the lesbian, gay, bisexual, or transgender parents in parenting their children. The more assistance straight spouses receive to work through disclosure issues constructively, the more likely they will gain a wider perspective and view their spouses or former spouses as partners in parallel parenting.

Besides getting peer support to resolve issues and to discern the reality of their particular situations, both spouses need to move beyond those first tumultuous years after the disclosure before they write their parenting plan in stone. "Two Minor Miracles," a story from *The Other Side of the Closet*, illustrates the importance of taking time for oneself alongside finding peer support. When Wes's wife came out, the pastor in their church announced her disclosure from the pulpit. Wes then lost his deaconship, and their son was told by the youth minister that his mother was going to hell. Devastated and angry at losing his wife's intimacy, now shared with her lover, Wes walked the streets nightly to rid his anger and sobbed in the shower so his children would not hear him and be further upset. He then found a local support group, and at the first meeting realized his pain was a human reaction to rejection, not a personal lesbian-versus-straight battle. Over time, with peer help, Wes discovered two miracles: His wife was still the same wonderful friend she had been and was still a good mother to their children. Wes and his wife now live a few blocks apart, their children free to go back and forth as they wish, with a bedroom, books, and toys in each of their homes.

I believe that, given peer support, factual information, and time to face and accept the situation, such miracles can become realistic possibilities for more mixed-orientation parents who divorce after disclosure.

The Straight Spouse Network may be reached at http://www.ssnetwk.org.

All in the Family
by James C. Johnstone

You are in your early 20s. It's Christmas. You have bused it from the safe preserve of a downtown gay ghetto to have dinner with your family. Your mom and dad, your elder sister and her redneck homophobic husband and their two-year-old son, your younger brother and his mousy bride, and a visiting aunt and uncle or two are gathered in your parents' shag-carpeted, split-level, very suburban hetero home to do the family thing: to have a nice Christmas dinner together.

For the last hour or so you've been playing horsey with your nephew to take his mind off the gleaming presents piled high under the gaily decorated spruce tree. The luscious aromas of turkey, gravy, stuffing, spruce boughs, and bayberry candles fill the house. It's five minutes to dinner, and your sister wants to talk to you. In private.

You slip away from the family, under the watchful eye of her hateful husband, whose big furry hands now hover protectively on your nephew's shoulders, restraining him. You follow your sister to your old bedroom, wondering what this is all about. She clears her throat but doesn't look you in the eye.

This is serious. In less than two minutes she blurts it all out. That she and (let's call him) Brutus have had a talk and reached a decision: that they are uncomfortable with you touching their son, your nephew. That it would be the best for all concerned if you stay away from him from now on.

There it is. The bomb has dropped, and you've been blasted speechless. Your sister finally meets your gaze, for a split second, and with a weak smile says, "I think Mom's calling us for dinner. Let's head back to the party," oblivious to the impact of the bomb she has dropped, the depth of the damage done. You are too stunned to respond. You go back to the party and have dinner with the family. Your sister and brother-in-law don't look at you. You avoid looking at your nephew. You skip dessert, leave early, say you have to catch a bus, and head out to another party. You forget to take your presents.

From that moment on you cut yourself off from any contact with your only nephew. From that moment on you do not speak to your sister. From that moment on you decide you don't have a sister; you never had one. And from that moment on you can never touch children again, let alone be around them without feeling self-conscious, watched, dirty, and dangerous.

This is a true story. It happened to my partner. Well, my ex-partner and current housemate, my friend Keith.

Nineteen years have passed since this family gathering took place. Brother and sister haven't spoken to each other since then. The times when Keith's family has a holiday gathering, it is always in two sessions—gay brother and estranged sister are never invited to the same party. Nephew and gay uncle haven't seen each other since that fateful night. This nephew—and my ex's father has said this often enough for it probably to be true—displays the same reserved, gentle character and the same book reader's lack of interest in sports or hunting (until he's forced into it by his homo-hating father) that Keith displayed when he was a teenager. They supposedly look alike, and the nephew's probably gay. If he is, he has endured 21 years in the protective talons of a father who swears he'd "fucking strangle the faggot" if he found out any son of his was a fairy. So much for fatherhood and family values.

Luckily, not all straight sisters and brothers are like my ex's; all is not doom and gloom on the family front. For every mean and narrow-minded bigot in our lives, there are straight family members whose matter-of-fact acceptance, open-mindedness, generosity of heart, and bottom-line blood-is-thicker-than-water attitude ("You're family, damn it!") go a long way to make up for the damage done by the fear and ignorance of homophobes in our midst.

I am lucky. My straight brother was supportive of me during my difficult coming-out process. (Royal Canadian Mounted Police officer father. You get the picture.) In fact, we are closer now since I've come out—and our lives have diverged—than we were growing up. Better still, my brother married a woman whose sister is gay.

Seven years ago my brother and sister-in-law had a baby boy. It had been a difficult pregnancy; my sister-in-law has Crohn's disease. The day after my nephew was born my ex and I went to visit her at the hospital. We were two gay men in the sanctum sanctorum of heterosexual pride and privilege: the maternity ward. My sister-in-law, still puffy and bloated from complications endured during the last weeks of her pregnancy, lay propped up in bed cradling a quivering bundle. My nephew was making the cutest little squeaking sounds.

"Do you want to hold him?"

Frankly, I was a little scared. I hesitated, then gingerly and clumsily gathered up the flannel-swaddled baby. It was an awesome moment. Tears filled my eyes. At the same time, I was deathly afraid I was holding him wrong, that I might be hurting him, or that I'd drop him.

I held him for a few minutes. The baby squeaked and fussed

in my embrace. I looked at Keith, who looked back at me and the baby with a mix of wonder, longing, and hesitation. I remembered the story of that family Christmas of long ago.

"Do you want to hold him?" I asked. "You're his uncle too, you know."

Keith hesitated, but I could see the look of eagerness in his eyes. He reached out and carefully took the squirming baby. I wondered how Keith would do. The funny thing was, as soon as he took my nephew in his arms the little baby looked up into his face, grabbed hold of Keith's finger, and stopped squirming. He relaxed, fell quiet, let out a big yawn, then fell asleep.

"Looks like you'll do just fine, uncle," my sister-in-law said.

My ex glowed all the way home.

Blood may be thicker than water, but it's clear that from the moment my nephew looked into my ex's face, some special bonding began. Just fine?! Over the past seven years my nephew Kyle has developed a bond with my ex that is as strong, if not stronger and closer, than the one the child has with me. I don't mind. Not really. Well, except for that time during the first critical weeks when my nephew was learning to talk and started using my ex's name to denote both of us. The more we laughed at it, the more he was encouraged to use it. For those couple of weeks "Keith" meant "uncle."

My nephew Kyle has brought a lot of healing into our lives. We have learned, all over again, what it means to be a family, the importance and rewards of being uncles—out gay uncles—and just how important it is for Kyle to be brought up in a family in which he learns that there are all sorts of people in this world, with different ways of living and loving. To see that he has options.

It has been wonderful to witness how Keith's relationship with Kyle has given Keith confidence and motivation to be more active and involved with the twin sons of his younger brother. After years of holding back, my ex has reclaimed his role as uncle and now spends fun, quality time with his nephews. Who knows? Cousins talk. Maybe someday my ex will be able to reconnect with his other nephew, so wrongfully and tragically torn from his life at that family Christmas long ago.

Years ago I thought children would never play a significant role in my life. I thought gay people had a destiny and a calling that was totally separate and outside the bounds of family and child raising. I called heterosexuals "breeders," and I couldn't understand lesbians and gay men who wanted to raise children. I didn't dislike children so much as I felt disassociated from them. Children logically belonged to the realm of heterosexuals, to people who had families. And didn't we have better things to do? Little did I know just how profoundly my relationship with my nephew would change all that for me.

Shortly after my nephew's second birthday I received a phone call from a stranger, a young lesbian named Laura (a friend of a friend of my ex) who was looking for a sperm donor. She wanted to meet a gay man with whom she was compatible and with whom she felt comfortable. Someone who would be interested in being an involved donor. Not a full coparent, mind you, but not an uninvolved, anonymous entity either.

The idea intrigued me. More accurately, it freaked me out because for the year or so prior three different psychics in a row had told me they saw I had a preexisting contract with a spirit to "provide it with a female body." The first time I heard it I was perplexed; I thought it was a psychic glitch. The reader knew I was gay and must have interpreted what she saw incorrectly. After the second and third readings by different psychics, however, I was even more puzzled, and wondered what "fulfilling" this contract might entail. Who was this spirit waiting for me to help provide it with a female body? The spirit of a long-lost friend? A lover or family member from a past life? Perhaps someone I knew who had died of AIDS? Did

I really have the wherewithal to be a father to this life I would help bring into the world? And who the heck was the mother? When I talked to Laura that first time on the phone all I could hear was the theme music from *The Twilight Zone* echoing in my head.

What followed was a half-year getting-to-know-you period. We discussed our families and our backgrounds, debated parenting philosophies, and talked about custody and relationship agreements. Would we actually write something down? Get lawyers involved? As far as either of us knew, no matter what we wrote, it would not hold much weight in a court of law.

After seven months of discussion and two blood tests I decided to go ahead with it—on trust. It just felt right. As if it were a natural progression, the logical next step. After all, who was I to back out on a preexisting spiritual contract? I trusted that whatever happened, whatever agreement we hammered out, this was all meant to be and that the details would look after themselves—and they have.

Today I have a beautiful five-year-old daughter named Jayka. I am part of an extended and diverse community of adults bonded by a commitment to help Laura and her coparenting friend, Cathy, raise Jayka in a loving and supportive family environment.

This family includes both gay and straight people, blood relatives, and friends. It includes my family: my parents, who consider Jayka their granddaughter; my brother and sister-in-law, who consider Jayka their niece; my nephew Kyle, who proudly points and calls out whenever he sees her, "That's my cousin Jayka"; and my ex, Jayka's second father. Jayka's family includes gay men and lesbians—some of them living as far away as Toronto and San Francisco, some who have never even met Jayka or Laura—who proudly claim their uncle and aunt statuses through their connections with one member or another of her Vancouver family.

After Jayka was born Keith and I moved to a house in east

Vancouver, in part to be closer to Jayka and Laura. Every Thursday for the first year or so, Keith and I would take Jayka for six hours while Laura went to work. We went for long walks with Jayka in her stroller. We learned to feed her, play with her, read to her, change her wet and dirty diapers, wipe the snot from her nose with our fingers when she had a cold, comfort her when she was crying, and sing lullabies to help her fall asleep.

During that time we were still "James" and "Keith," but sometime around Jayka's second birthday the "D" word began to be used—first by Cathy, then by Laura and others. Jayka began to call me "Dada," and she called Keith "Dee." She couldn't pronounce Ks for the longest time. I liked to joke that between Keith and me we made a complete "Dad-dy." Today Jayka calls me both Dad and James, and though she usually calls Keith by his name, she'll say "my dads" when referring to the two of us, and when talking to others about Keith she'll say "my other dad."

It's funny—when I first heard her talking like this in front of the neighborhood kids I felt odd, a bit apprehensive. I wondered how these children from what I expected to be traditional nuclear families would react. To my utter astonishment I heard two older twin girls respond with envy. "Two dads? You're lucky. We don't even have one dad." The twins, I found out later, were adopted. My fear vanished. In its stead I felt relief mixed with sadness, and more than a little shame at my earlier defensive attitude.

Jayka is a miracle I never expected to happen in my life. And miracles continue to occur. For the first couple of years that we lived in the East End, Laura and Jayka moved four times. Sometimes they moved closer to our house, sometimes farther away. I worried about how the moves would affect Jayka, particularly her ability to make and sustain friendships. I especially resented the second-to-last move that took Jayka and her family miles away, a great psychological distance considering that Keith and I don't have a car. But then the house directly behind ours became available, and I told Laura about it. She and her roommates applied for tenancy and were accepted. Today our backyards adjoin one another, separated only by a picket fence.

Very often, when I wake up and open my bedroom window blinds, I will look out to her house and see Jayka smiling and excitedly waving to me from her kitchen window or bouncing on her trampoline in her backyard. Often she will just drop by, sometimes by herself or sometimes with a whole pack of friends in tow. Since Laura and Jayka moved here, it seems that our neighborhood has sprouted many kids her age, some—miracle of miracles—complete with queer parents!

Jayka now comes over for regular overnight stays. During our time together Keith and I try our best to be good dads, supporting and encouraging, nurturing and teaching, listening and loving. And we learn from Jayka as much as we teach her. We play and cook together; so far I have taught her to bake muffins, soda biscuits, and bread with me. She loves to help with the cooking and household chores, and also helps with gardening. She can identify all the edible herbs throughout the garden and sometimes scares the daylights out of unsuspecting adult visitors who see her reach out and pop a strange leaf into her mouth. "It's only sage," she assures them, wondering what all the fuss is about.

I'm trying to pass on to Jayka all the things I thought were important from my childhood: a love of reading and story-telling; traditional lullabies and folk songs at bedtime; a respect for homemade bread, along with my mother's Prince Edward Island brown-bread recipe; a love of gardening and growing vegetables and herbs; an appreciation for birds and wild animals and their environment; the study of ancient history, diverse cultures, and spiritualities; and an interest in learning other languages. Of course, she will develop her own interests and set her own course of studies and path as she grows older, but right now I want to expose her to as many different things, ideas, and opportunities as I can.

I am delighted to see how Jayka uses her imagination as well as the amazing self-confidence she demonstrates time and again. I can't help believe she is so strong in these areas because of the amazing resources and models she can draw upon from her large and diverse alternative family and all the love, care, attention, and encouragement we provide her. If this is how she is heading into kindergarten, what is she going to be like when she's all grown up?

Everything I have observed—everything I have experienced around lesbians and gay men relating to children and creating family—flies in the face of the religious right's malicious lies, vicious fear- and hate-mongering, and homophobic propaganda. My ex's sister's son didn't and doesn't need protection from his gay uncle. The irony and the tragedy is that he probably needs to be protected from his heterosexual father.

Let the narrow-minded, the homophobes, and the religious right continue to circle their wagons around the ever-diminishing and impoverished definition of the traditional family and what family values are supposed to be. Lesbians and gay men are quietly and bravely reclaiming our ability to be family, to raise families, and to be proud and visible. We are loving, nurturing, stable, and honest parents (or uncles, or aunts)—role models and caregivers for the new millennium's children. We're busy making families that are slowly but inevitably going to change and inherit the world.

Beyond the White Picket Fence
by Rachel Pepper

Every few months at the house of my girlfriend "B" another newspaper clipping appears. It's usually sitting on top of a pile of papers, a gift from the friendly neighbor across the street. When I spot it I grit my teeth and gingerly peruse it when B's not in the room. Yep, it's one more sad story from our local newspaper about a nonbiological mother losing custody of "her" kids. The woeful face of the non–bio mom peers up at me from her photograph, pictures of the children surrounding her, her tragic tale laid out in the columns of text that follow. I sigh. The story is always the same, just one more variation on a new but thoroughly overplayed theme.

I know B's neighbor's intent is good. He does mean well, and I don't think he aims to hurt my feelings per se. He's friends with B, and he wants her to know about this stuff. Even though he's a straight bachelor in his 60s with no children of his own, he's quite interested in the legalities of lesbian relationships, especially those in which there is a child. Our child. My child. Yes, from his safe vantage point across the street, behind his own picket fence, B's neighbor feels free to throw newspaper-clipping barbs.

Almost two years ago I gave birth to a daughter, Frances, the result of 15 years of my yearning. Of a need that marked itself everywhere in my life, that made itself clear in a thousand tiny ways. In the endless hours spent baby-sitting as a teen. In the friendships I had with many children in my life, including the small boy who sometimes slipped and called me "Mom." In the parenting magazine subscriptions that flooded my mailbox. In the box of baby clothes stored forever on a closet's high shelf. In the endless discussions with friends about babies in general and my future one in particular. It was a need that absolutely, resolutely had to be fulfilled.

By the time I met B the quiet need hidden well under the surface of my everyday life had evolved into a roar pushing through my skin. Past lovers had shied away from the baby thing, but B was sympathetic and urged me to try to conceive. What her role was, we couldn't yet fathom. We had only been together a few months when I registered at the sperm bank, but as I took those first steps toward conception B was by my side. She didn't participate fully, but she encouraged me, and she was there.

Already, though, we were existing within a different paradigm from the normal lesbian mode. The rules for our particular situation weren't yet written. We certainly did not fit the description of the typical lesbian couple trying to have a child. We had been partners for less than a year. I was not going to be a single parent, yet we couldn't really say we had planned this baby together. We did not know what having a child meant to us as a couple. We hadn't worked through any of the issues that arise when couples make a baby, such as spousal support, day care, college funds, or what the baby would call each of us. We did not live together, have a joint banking account, or even a matching wardrobe. I have never had a joint checking account. I have never owned a house. No one has ever supported me. In short, I have never expected much from anyone and usually do not know how to ask. I have always been a poor candidate for the white-picket-fence crowd.

You know what I mean when I talk about the white-picket-fence gals. They're the vanilla girls who hide in the suburbs, too scared or unhip to live an urban existence. All they want to be is normal…whatever that means! They've usually been together forever. Everything is duly shared. They have a child to fill the empty bedroom in the house behind the white picket fence. They are the types of gay folk that nasty street activists like myself differentiated ourselves from in the early '90s by calling ourselves "queer." And while times have changed (and so have I), that rosy ideal of pseudo-heterosexual norms still haunts the white-picket-fence crowd.

So B and I were, by extension, suspect. And because I was the one who so desperately wanted a child, and because I was the one who got pregnant, and because I was the one who popped out the baby, I was the most suspect. And I guess, if you ask folks such as B's neighbor across the street, I still am. And since B is the nonbiological parent in our particular family kingdom she is obviously the one these articles, in their simple-minded portrayal of someone else's family drama, could someday be about.

Of course, I read every one of the newspaper clippings the neighbor provides. Not surprisingly, these articles bring out extremely strong, fully mixed emotions in me. A typical story goes something like this: A lesbian couple plans a baby together, and Mommy A gives birth. There have been many promises that Mommy A will never *ever* deny Mommy B from seeing the baby. A year after the baby's born, the women break up. (Surprise, surprise: Having a child is harder than anyone imagined, and their perfect lesbian relationship has crumbled!) Of course, since Mommy A is doing all the work of childbearing, the baby lives with her. She decides she doesn't want Mommy B so involved and limits Mommy B's participation. Mommy B pushes for partial custody and loses in the admittedly homophobic court system. Mommy A doesn't let Mommy B see the baby anymore, and Mommy B phones reporters. OK, so I've oversimplified, but Mommy B's supporters are on a rampage and really want you to believe that Mommy A—the *biological mother*—is the monster that must be punished with publicity.

Me, I always wonder what the newspaper reports don't print. I wonder if Mommy B really wanted that baby the way Mommy A always did. I wonder if she clamored to make a baby or if she just went along for the ride. I wonder if she was kind to the biological mother, before and after her pregnancy. I wonder if she made a good spouse. I wonder if she helped equally with the baby and contributed equal funds to the baby's upkeep. I wonder if she fooled around on the bio mom when she was pregnant or pressured her for sex afterward when she wasn't in the mood. I wonder if she yelled at her or hit her. I wonder if Mommy B ever bothered to change a diaper, clean the cat box, get up in the night and rock the baby, or let the biological mother sleep in for a change. I wonder if she went out cavorting with her friends while the biological mother was chained to a nursing baby at home. I wonder: Does she just want the goodies that go along with parenthood, without all the sacrifice? I wonder if Mommy B understood at all what it meant to be a mother; was ready to sacrifice all to be a mother; if she really tried hard to be one.

In case you're wondering, most of these are not my own issues. But I know plenty of horror stories from biological moms in which partners lie, cheat, don't pay a penny toward the baby, don't get up in the night, and basically don't do their share despite all the pre-baby promises they made. There is nothing in those newspaper clippings about that. I wonder when the other side of the story will be portrayed. I have a feeling that no reporter is interested in the lack of equity in sleep deprivation between comothers. Lawsuits from victimized nonbiological mothers make better copy.

One day I tell B that these newspaper clippings make me uncomfortable, that they make me feel suspect, even accused. Her reply is that it is important for her to know about these things. That she is glad the neighbor brings them over. That I shouldn't take it personally. But how, I wonder, can I not? It's not nice to be thought of as suspect. It's not nice to know others see you as the one who holds all the power and, therefore, the one who can be hurtful. It's not nice to be thought of as *the one who could take the baby away*.

It's not like I would ever want to keep B away from Frances. They so obviously adore one another in a love affair borne not of biology but of their own free will. They chose to love one another and have nurtured that love in many ways. Through kisses and hugs and tender words. Through many hours spent at the zoo petting the goats. Through silly play sessions with the crazy toys only B would buy her, such as a mutant monster named Crush Me Phil. And, of course, through a shared passion for shortbread cookies. I acknowledge their love to myself and others, and also acknowledge it legally in my will, which names B as the baby's guardian should I die. I would not want to be pushed to pull Frances out of B's world. But I still want to claim the right to do so.

After all, I am still the baby's mother. She sprang from me; she is of me and my body. While she is her own separate entity and her destiny is quite apart from mine, I did have a large hand in her creation. I asked her to come, and kept trying till she did. Her physical and intellectual capacities are drawn from me and, of course, from her biological father, who is not involved in raising her. While my partner has a big influence on Frances, she is not "of" her. Frances did not grow in her belly, did not share her body. She did not push out of her cooch. She did not suckle at her breast. She was created by me, nurtured by me, and is of me. This is not something that can be denied. And if I ever want to move across the world and take the baby with me, I don't want anyone telling me I can't. Ever.

The woman who was my midwife is a lesbian and has worked with many lesbian couples. She differentiates in her own mind about the differing roles two women play in choosing to have a baby. Even though many couples make no distinction in their roles, "J" states quite adamantly that "one woman is the mother, and the other is the mother's partner." It is very clear to her that the one who births the baby is the mom. The mom makes the baby. That is what mothers do. It is the same way for her when she sees straight couples. If a soon-to-be dad gets too pushy with his views about how the mom should give birth, J is always there to remind him—gently, of course—that he is not the one pushing a baby out his cooch. There is still a difference in how men and women are created and in how they create. It may be easier that way. Too much equality among women, it seems, can only lead to conflict or, at least, confusion. And lawsuits.

Many days I feel confused myself. I feel confused about my ambiguities and about why I can't be trusting like most lesbians I know. I certainly love B with all my heart. She is my best friend, my perfect companion. We have both expressed to the other that we feel married in all the best senses of the word, though our relationship, compared with other lesbians, is certainly unconventional.

Often I would rather be innocently oblivious to mistakes I could make, bumbling through life like most folks, making stupid choices in a haze of good intentions. Trouble is, a year or two later such people find themselves on *Judge Judy* wondering how everything went so horribly wrong. I am too cynical—and, I'd say, too smart—to find myself in that place. I don't want to end up on *Judge Judy*. I don't want to be a statistic in the National Center for Lesbian Rights parenting dossier. I don't want to be a clipping cut out from the newspaper. And so I guard myself and, by extension, my baby. We three are a family, and we are not. We exist uneasily in this quandary, and we wait for it to change.

The big issue in the lesbian parenting world these days is co-adoption. Specifically, this means the adoption by the non-biological mom of her partner's biological kids. There are many examples of how such a law is both necessary and useful: in the case of foreign adoption, say, in which both women start from an equal place and need protection in jointly raising their children. To assist in estate planning. To provide full medical benefits to a sick child who is not biologically one's own. To prove to relatives that the family is real, in social and legal terms, even if it is not real to prejudiced eyes. And, I might add, to legitimize our families to ourselves.

Still, such a serious legal tactic is not for everyone and should not be the standard to which everyone has to live. I have often felt like the mean biological mother around my coupled friends for not allowing B to co-adopt Frances. They don't get that while co-adoption is becoming "the norm" among lesbian families in California, it is only their norm, not mine. Co-adoption has become the great divide by which we measure our families—the legal "right side" of the tracks, if you will, where "real" lesbian families can now gloat over the rest of us. There is no sense of irony among these women that after fighting for years to be different from the heterosexual nuclear norm, they have succeeded in replicating it. Not only that, women who balk at the implications of co-adoption for their own situations are made to feel demonized.

I resent the implication of this. Often, when I hear the biological mothers in my play group talk about going through the co-adoption process with their lovers, I have to stop myself from shouting, "Don't do it!" I know they would claim that they planned their children together, so these children are theirs together. But I wonder if they realize they are signing away their sole legal rights to the child they bore—forever. That now they can never again make an autonomous decision about that child. That they cannot cross an international border now without permission from their lover. That they are now linked to this other woman, legally, for the duration of their entire lives. I've seen enough heterosexual marriages falter to know the horrors of divorce firsthand. Through co-adoption, lesbians too will be participating in these horrors firsthand. Think lesbians are immune to messy breakups? Think about your own life. Think about the screaming matches, the jealousies, the torn-up pictures, the fights over the cat. Now think about having to share a child forever, long after the flame is gone and the relationship's down the tubes. Now think about happily coparenting a growing child—forever.

I know in some circles this kind of talk makes me an asshole, a renegade, a person who is not to be trusted. A cynic of the worst order, and no friend of lesbians. I know I belong to a small, greedy minority that wants to have their cake and eat it too, and this does not make me proud. I wish I could throw away all my reservations and treat child rearing like I was buying a condo or SUV: equal input, equal access. The fact that I cannot does not make me popular among my white-picket friends, who foolishly believe they will all be together forever, blissfully raising their babies. It also makes me feel especially guilty in my own relationship, since my partner has done a complete turnaround since Frances was born and has indicated that she would like to be a full, legally responsible coparent. I'm just not ready to let her be. At the same time, I resent that she gets to make that choice. When you birth a baby, you do not.

I know I want something that hasn't yet existed, that perhaps can't (by its very nature) exist. In my utopian universe we would love Frances equally, but the baby would always love me more. In my utopian universe the biological mother would always have more. More rights. More respect. More love. More chance of being called "Momma" first and having that name stick. I know this makes me different, but surely I cannot be alone. I know there must be other women out there, either partnered or coupled, whose children came from their own singular desire to birth them, yet who have somehow entered into a new kind of family pact with their partners once the baby was born. Who are not yet ready to erase all that came before but are already living another reality. Who are waiting for the two worlds to meld. Stuck in a lesbian family nether-world shy of one thing, short of the other. Yes, I can relate. That's where I find myself these days.

And yet there's a part of me that longs for the white picket fence. I want to park myself behind it, smugly smirking out at the world. *See,* I want to say, *see what I made for myself. See how happy I am here, safe in my little cocoon of domesticity, far from the madding crowds of queerdom. See how well we've done, my partner and I, in creating this for ourselves, while you losers mill around outside, seeking this very kind of life.* Some days it seems so within my reach.

Yes, I do feel the white picket fence calling me sometimes. After all, there's nothing like having a partner who loves your baby as much as you do. Or maybe, some days, even more, since B can never take that love, even for a second, for grant-ed. It's a secret society that only we can enter, this world of Frances worship—where no one else can ever love Frances or care as much about her future as we do. There's no one else besides B who is there in a second if Frances is sick or whose welcoming door I can knock on in the middle of the night to say, "Here we are. Please take us in." There is nothing better than the fun times we spend together as a family, whatever it is we are doing. And there is no one else but B to whom I automatically turn, knowing she'll meet my eyes to acknowl-edge that, yes, we have the most incredible, most gorgeous, most smart-as-a-whip, go-get-'em, baby-tiger-little-Leo girl who ever lived. This is what makes us a family no matter how you define it. And I know I'm damn lucky to have this.

So here is what I hope for. Someday B and I will have worked through all our issues and embrace life together as one but still as two. We will live together in a great huge house, big enough for a bunch of outgoing, independent, stubborn, and strong souls to happily coexist. We will have separate checking accounts and probably a joint one too. Frances will have two parents who pay the bills, care for her every need, and always make her laugh, whether they're called Momma (that's me) or not (that's B). We will fill the house with the much-discussed, much-longed-for children waiting for us out there somewhere and the dogs and cats who claim us. And always, always, we will have each other.

And if you look carefully enough underneath the veneer of this jaded, cantankerous queer, you will see the glimmer of a white picket fence calling me home.

Contributors

Laurie Bell's work includes *Mourn and Organize: A Collected Remembrance of World AIDS Day* (Exhibit, 1997); *Good Girls/Bad Girls: Sex Trade Workers and Feminists Face to Face* (Women's Press, 1987); *On Our Own Terms: A Practical Guide for Lesbian and Gay Relationships* (CLGRO, 1991); and *No Safe Bed: LGBT Youth and Residential Services* (CTYS, 1993).

Terry Boggis, one of the founding members of Center Kids (New York), now serves as its director. Center Kids is the largest regional alternative-families program in the country. Prior to her position with Center Kids, Terry was the Lesbian and Gay Community Services Center's director of communications, the last of several positions she held during her 15 years as a corporate and nonprofit communications specialist. Her work has been published in *The New York Times* and a number of lesbian family publications.

Susie Bright is the author/editor of 14 books, including *Full*

Exposure: Opening Up to Sexual Creativity and Erotic Expression and *The Best American Erotica* series. She can be found online at: http://www.susiebright.com.

Amity Pierce Buxton, Ph.D., director of the Straight Spouse Network and board member of Family Pride Coalition, wrote *The Other Side of the Closet: The Coming-Out Crisis for Straight Spouses and Families* and "The Best Interest of Children of Gay and Lesbian Parents" in *The Scientific Basis of Child Custody Decisions*, edited by Robert M. Galatzer-Levy and Louis Kraus.

Loree Cook-Daniels is an activist and writer whose work has appeared in the *Washington Blade*; outonthenet.com; *Lesbians Raising Sons*; *Looking Queer: Body Image and Identity in Lesbian, Bisexual, Gay and Transgender Communities*; and *Trans Forming Families: Real Stories About Transgendered Loved Ones*.

LauRose Felicity *lives* transracial family. She has been taught the meaning of loyalty and wonder in statements such as this by her mother-in-law, Ruth (in notable Southern drawl): "If anyone was rude to my grandbaby just because she's black, why, I'd just have to kill him." At age 72 Granny Ruth moved from Louisiana to San Francisco with Ms. Felicity and her family. She is now is an activist for lesbian families.

Jenifer J. Firestone, LCSW, founded Alternative Family Matters in Cambridge, Mass., has for the past ten years helped hundreds of lesbians and gay men through the complex process of having children, and has also assisted medical and community institutions to better understand and serve lesbian- and gay-headed families. She is a passionate and eternally hopeful skeptic with a six-year-old daughter whom she coparents with two gay men.

Aimee Gelnaw's longtime queer family activism includes organizing Lambda Families in New Jersey and Rainbow Families in Chicago. She is a cochair of the Family Pride Coalition and one of the authors of *Opening Doors: Lesbian and Gay Parents and Schools*.

Tzivia Gover, of Ashfield, Mass., received her MFA in creative nonfiction from Columbia University. Her articles have appeared in *The Boston Globe*, *Poets & Writers*, *The Christian Science Monitor*, and many other publications. She has written about lesbian and gay parenting issues for the anthology *Lesbians Raising Sons*; *Family: A Celebration*, edited by Margaret Campbell; *The Advocate*; and other gay and lesbian publications.

Judy Grahn teaches in MA and MFA programs at New College of California in women's spirituality and writing-and-consciousness programs. She has a Ph.D. in women's spirituality and a Lifetime Achievement Award in lesbian literature. Search the Web, especially http://www.serpentina.com, for more info.

James Hughson has a master's degree in psychology from the California Institute for Integral Studies. At Alternative Family Project he worked with adults, families, and children, and co-led a gay fathers group, a gay and lesbian parents group, and others.

Arlene Istar Lev is a family therapist who specializes in working with the lesbian, gay, bisexual, and transgender communities. She is an educator, trainer, grassroots activist, and writer committed to making this world a safe home for queer families.

Kimberly Mistysyn is an American-born Canadian mother, writer, and once-upon-a-time publisher and editor. Her son and partner bring continuous joy to her life. Her son's fathers are a wonderful and unique extension of their family.

James C. Johnstone's work has been included in the anthologies *Sister & Brother: Lesbians and Gay Men Write About Their Lives Together* and *Flashpoints: Gay Male Sexual Writing* as well as in *Prairie Fire, Icon Magazine,* and *The Buzz.* He has edited several short-fiction anthologies, including the *Queer View Mirror* series, with Karen X. Tulchinksy, and the series *Quickies: Short Short Fiction on Gay Male Desire.* James lives in Vancouver, Canada.

Rachel Pepper gave birth twice in the last few years: once to a beautiful, spirited daughter named Frances and once to her book, *The Ultimate Guide to Pregnancy for Lesbians* (Cleis, 1999). She believes parenting is the ultimate emotional, physical, and spiritual challenge and that it may well be the queer community's final frontier.

Marcia Perlstein, a marriage family therapist, has been practicing in Berkeley, Calif., and San Francisco since 1967. She is the clinical director of Alternative Family Project in San Francisco and director of the Lesbian Therapist Referral Service.

Cindy Rizzo is a lesbian mother, writer, and activist from Boston. She and her ex-partner had joint custody of their two sons, ages 7 and 13 at the time the piece was written. Her work can be found in *Lesbians Raising Sons, All The Ways Home: Parenting and Children in the Lesbian and Gay Communities* (which she coedited), *Gay Community News; Sojourner,* and *The New York Times.*

Sarah Schulman is the author of eight novels, including *The Child* (forthcoming); *Shimmer* (Avon, 1998); *Rat Bohemia*

(Dutton, 1995), winner of the Ferro-Grumley Prize for lesbian fiction and a finalist for the Prix de Rome; *Empathy* (Dutton, 1992); *People in Trouble* (Dutton, 1990), winner of the Gregory Kolovakos Award for AIDS Fiction; *After Delores* (Dutton, 1988), winner of the American Library Association's Gay, Lesbian and Bisexual Book Award for fiction; *Girls, Visions, and Everything* (Seal, 1986); *The Sophie Horowitz Story* (Naiad, 1984); the novella *The Mere Future* (forthcoming); and two nonfiction books, *My American History: Lesbian and Gay Life During the Reagan/Bush Years* (Routledge, 1994), winner of the Gustavus Meyer Award for a Work Promoting Tolerance; and *Stagestruck: Theater, AIDS, and the Marketing of Gay America* (Duke University Prize, 1999), winner of the American Library Association's Gay, Lesbian and Bisexual Book Award for nonfiction.

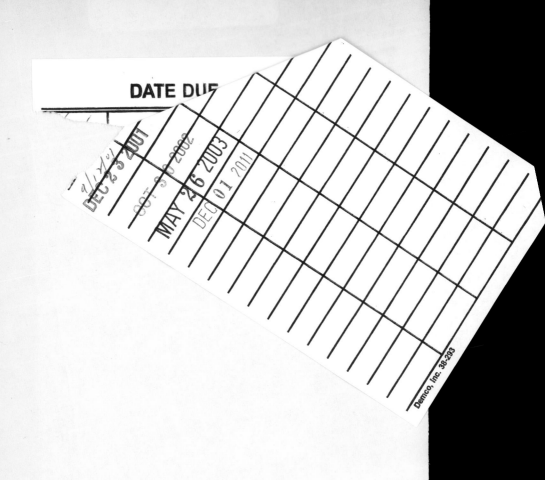